ANTIQUE
STYLE

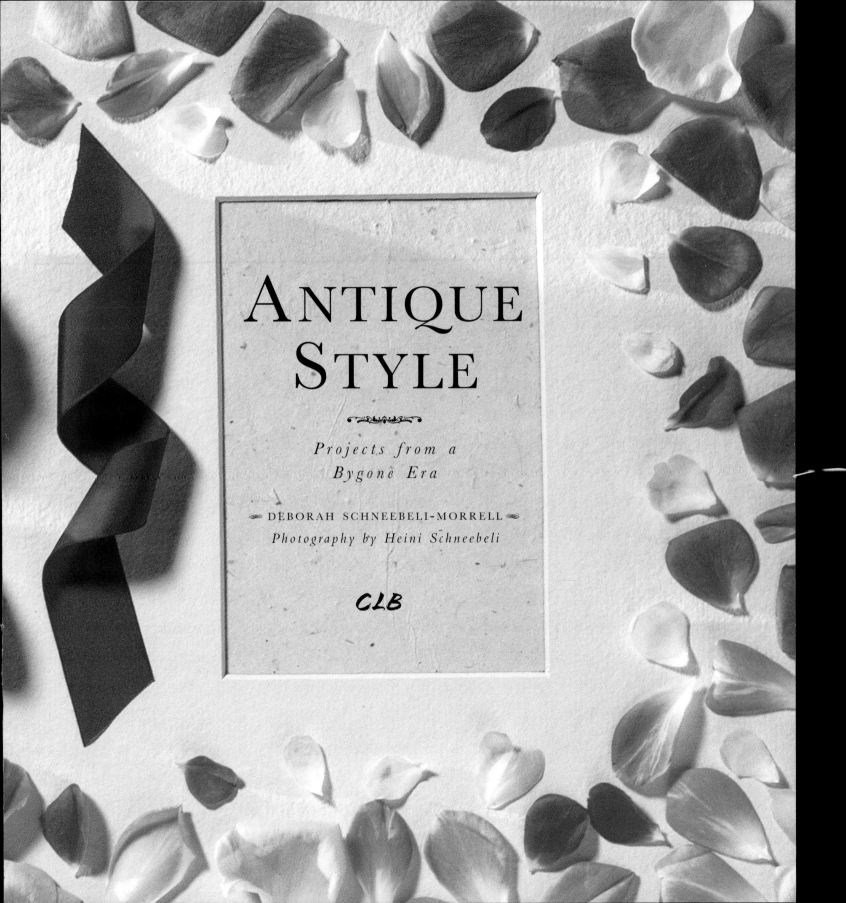

ANTIQUE STYLE

Projects from a Bygone Era

DEBORAH SCHNEEBELI-MORRELL

Photography by Heini Schneebeli

CLB

Antique Style

Designed and created by

THE BRIDGEWATER BOOK COMPANY LTD

Art Director: Peter Bridgewater
Designer: Jane Lanaway
Editor: Geraldine Christy
Managing Editor: Mandy Greenfield
Photography: Heini Schneebeli
Page make-up: Chris Lanaway

5037 Antique Style – Projects from a Bygone Era
This edition published in 1997 by CLB
Distributed in the U.S.A. by BHB International, Inc.
30 Edison Drive, Wayne, New Jersey 07470
© 1997 CLB International
Printed and bound in Singapore
ISBN 1–85833–800–X

CONTENTS

CONTENTS

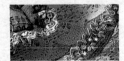

CONTENTS

INTRODUCTION

W E ALL LOOK back with affection and nostalgia to Victorian times; indeed, most people probably have one or two items in their homes today that were made or collected by their grandparents or great-grandparents. Victorian crafts were initially very much in the domain of middle-class ladies. The Industrial Revolution had created a class of newly rich who were able to employ servants and had time on their hands. This led to a flowering of domestic creativity in all sorts of areas. Watercolor painting, embroidery and needlework, calligraphy, papercrafts, and flower arranging were all skills which Victorian ladies acquired. Today we marvel at their inventiveness and technical ability.

Fashionable ladies' magazines published articles on household management and etiquette, as well as providing patterns and inspiration for all kinds of handcrafts. In the spirit of those publications, this book gathers together dozens of charming and beautiful projects using materials both Victorian and modern so that you can recreate the domestic artistry of a more leisured age.

The Victorians were passionate about gardening. Botany was studied seriously in childhood, and pressing flowers was often the first craft a child learned. Ladies, in particular, avidly collected, pressed and assembled beautiful specimens from the garden into lovely floral albums enhanced by sentimental verse, watercolor paintings and accomplished penmanship. Flowers, grasses, leaves, and seed pods were picked, dried, and arranged into all manner of baskets, vases, and urns to grace the mantelpiece, drawing room, dining room, or parlor, and were arranged into bouquets, sprays, wreaths, buttonholes, and hair ornaments.

There are a lot of projects using flowers in this collection. You can press flowers very simply with a large heavy book and some absorbent paper to place your specimens between. The flowers can be used to prettify plain white candles, to make Valentine or birthday cards, or to decorate picture frames and mounts. Dried flowers are also the basis for many lovely decorative arrangements, as well as the classic and ubiquitous Victorian potpourri.

The favorite Victorian flowers were of course roses, the flowers of love and romance. Arranged into hearts or made into scented sachets, the preserved buds and petals could bring the breath of summer into the house all the year round. The other plant much favored by the Victorians was lavender, whose delightful scent they preserved in many ingenious ways. We have included projects which use lavender to make sweet-smelling furniture polish, fragrant clothes hangers and bags, and scented oils.

Découpage was a skill in which many Victorian ladies excelled. Using pretty paper scraps, little pictures, and lacy doilies, simple boxes could be transformed into beautiful gifts, or an ordinary photograph enhanced by a decorative frame. This technique can also be used to brighten up a plain lampshade. Trays and plates can also be decorated using this technique as long as you seal the pattern of glued scraps with some durable glaze.

Perhaps the most popular Victorian craft activity was needlework, an accomplishment which every lady acquired. Pillowcases, napkins, bags, quilts, even oven gloves can be made quite simply and decorated with braiding, buttons, ribbons, and of course lace. It is possible to find old lace in antique shops and at specialist market stalls, although luckily modern lace is often of a very high quality and indistinguishable in style and pattern from the real thing. Ribbons are also quite easy to obtain in a range of patterns and colors, and there are shops that carry reproductions of old designs. Thus it is possible to decorate and trim clothes and hats with materials that have a truly Victorian feel and appearance even though they are all modern.

The garden and the kitchen offered a wealth of creative opportunities. A well-stocked and maintained garden was essential not only for the supply of fruit and vegetables for the table, but also as a source of herbs and flowers for culinary

uses. We have gathered recipes for exotic Victorian favorites such as
Rhumtopf and rose petal jam, and traditional drinks for winter and
summer: comforting hot punch and eggnog, and refreshing elderflower
drinks. Herbs were used to make flavored oils and vinegars, and for
toiletries and perfumes, and these recipes are also
included here.

All these projects have been
inspired by the creative and inventive spirit
of the Victorian lady. The materials and
ingredients are all simple and readily
available, and with only a little diligence and
care you can delight your friends with handmade gifts and fill your home with beautiful
reminders of a bygone age.

C A N D L E S

*B*EFORE GAS for lighting was widely installed in Victorian homes, candles were used sparingly. The wax variety was generally used only in grander homes or when important guests were expected. Servants had to make do with tallow candles that smoked and sputtered uncontrollably. Candles were never left unattended and it was important to extinguish them at night to save the wax and protect the home from fire. Pressing flowers was a favorite activity of Victorian ladies, and here flowers are used to decorate candles. It only takes about two weeks to press flowers successfully. If you do not have a flower press just lay your specimens carefully between absorbent paper within the pages of a heavy book. When pressed, the following flowers and leaves are suitable for sticking onto candles: pansies, ferns, lavender, potentilla, primrose, hydrangeas, geranium, and any pretty small leaves.

M A T E R I A L S

Selection of dried flowers
Wax glue
Small double saucepan
Small paintbrush
Assortment of wax candles
Dipping can 3 × 8 in.
2 lb. paraffin wax
Deep saucepan

*J*ust a little candle, shining
in the dark,
Drives away the shadows with each tiny spark.

The Children's Friend
1895

1 Select the flowers you are going to use. If you decide to use leaves, make sure they are a little shorter than the candle.

2 Melt a small amount of the wax glue over hot water in a small double saucepan. With the small paintbrush put spots of glue onto the candle where the flowers will be placed. The glue dries quickly; press the flowers onto the candle while the glue is drying.

3 Continue gluing the flowers around the candle.

4 *Put the dipping can full of paraffin wax into a deep pan of very hot water. The wax will reduce as it melts.*

5 *Holding the candle by the wick, quickly dip it in and out of the hot wax; dip twice only so that the outer layer of wax is thin enough for the pressed flowers to show through.*

CAROL SERVICE

Many of the larger aristocratic country houses in England have their own adjoining private chapel. Here the servants were expected to attend family worship on Sunday. On Christmas Eve the entire household from above and below stairs, including any house guests present for the festivities, gathered for the candlelit carol service held in the late afternoon. This was a magical time for the occupants of the nursery quarters, especially if they had been involved in the decoration of the candles.

C̶andles were usually brought in with tea; but we only burnt one at a time. As we lived in constant preparation for a friend who might come in, any evening (but who never did), it required some contrivance to keep our candles of the same length, ready to be lighted, and to look as if we burnt two always.

Cranford
ELIZABETH GASKELL 1810–65

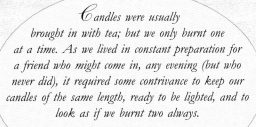

VIOLETS AND PANSIES

*V*IOLETS AND their close relatives, pansies and miniature violas, were particular favorites in the Victorian garden. The sweet violet is famous for its fragrance, which is used in perfumes, eau de Cologne and in scented lozenges to sweeten the breath. Pansies flower later than violets, their upturned smiling faces always a welcome sight at the front of a border. Pansies and violets are normally grown as biennials, but if the seeds are sown early enough they will flower later the same year.

TO GROW PANSIES FROM SEED

1 Sow the pansy seeds ¹/₁₆ in. deep in good seed compost in early spring. Cover to exclude light.

2 Keep the soil moist and fairly warm. Remove the cover when the seedlings appear.

3 Transplant the seedlings into trays spaced 2 in. apart, when they are large enough to handle. Grow on in good light.

4 Acclimatize plants to the outside gradually and after ten days transplant to their final flowering positions. These flowers are happily

TUSSIE MUSSIE

*T*he Tussie Mussie was a small, tightly bound hand-held posy of fragrant flowers. In the mid-nineteenth century it became popular as an accessory carried by fashionable ladies. When presented by an admirer it became a vehicle for the floral "language of love" in which symbolic messages were carried by the inclusion of certain flowers. The pansy meant "You are in my thoughts" and the violet stood for faithfulness. The herbs and flowers in this Tussie Mussie have been picked from an English cottage garden and include marigolds, feverfew, small roses, cornflowers, and pinks.

1 Start with a small posy in the middle and encircle it with a variety of contrasting herbs and flowers. Bind together as you go along with a reel of fine florists' wire.

2 Gradually build up the Tussie Mussie, adding different flowers. Space them evenly according to color; insert the leafy herbs among the flowers.

3 Encircle with an outer rim of small-leafed herbs such as rosemary or santolina. Bind to finish, cut the stems evenly and push a posie holder up so the lacy edge touches the flowers.

A violet by a mossy stone
Half hidden from the eye!
Fair as a star, when only one
Is shining in the sky

WILLIAM WORDSWORTH
1770–1850

HEARTS

M ANY VICTORIAN Valentines were extremely complicated; one dated 1846 showed a finely dressed gentleman whose waistcoat opened to reveal his heart, on which was a picture of his lady love. The family firm of Jonathan King was well known in the late 1800s for their highly decorated Valentines using wonderful combinations of tinsel, swansdown, glass beads, dried flowers, and pressed ferns.

VALENTINE

The main image in this unusual Valentine is the pressed heart-shaped leaf from which a smaller heart motif has been cut. Many leaves are heart-shaped; violets are perfect, if a little small. Pick them with the stalk still attached and press between absorbent paper within the leaves of a heavy book.

MATERIALS

Pressed large heart-shaped leaf

Off-white handmade paper

Pinking shears

Deep purple cardboard

Small scissors

Sharp soft pencil

Craft knife

Cutting mat

Small selection of pressed flowers and small ferns

Toothpicks for applying glue

Rubber-based glue for flowers

12 in. of purple rayon ribbon ½ in. wide

1 Lay the heart-shaped leaf on off-white paper and cut around it with pinking shears so that there is 1¼ in. extra at the sides, base and top of the leaf. Cut the purple cardboard ¾ in. larger than the background paper.

2 Cut a small heart shape from the off-cuts of the off-white paper. Lay it onto the center of the pressed leaf. Draw around it and cut it out with the craft knife; this should be done on a cutting mat.

3 Put the leaf in the center of the paper and arrange the other pressed flowers in a circlet around it; stick them in place. Choose a small matching flower to fit inside the cut-out heart. Use the toothpicks to dab small amounts of glue onto the paper where the flowers are to be stuck. Allow the glue to dry.

4 Cut two small slits either side of the stalk of the leaf. Thread the ribbon through and tie into a pretty bow. Then glue the whole onto the purple card so that a narrow border is visible.

❧ LOVE NOTES ❧

*W*ith the magical use of a photocopier it is easy to make a pretty collection of charming notelets. Tied together in sets with an attractive ribbon, they make a really special gift for an important person. If you do not have any ivory paper you can achieve an antiqued effect by painting white paper with tea; allow it to dry, then iron out any crinkles with a medium hot iron.

MATERIALS

Selection of black and white engravings of flower posies and decorative borders

Scissors

Paper glue

2 sheets of white paper 8 x 11 in.

5 sheets of ivory paper 8 x 11 in.

Colored ribbon

1 *Select an appealing black and white engraving of flowers. Cut it out and paste it onto white 8 x 11 in. paper.*

2 *Cut out a border and frame this image; the frame should be about $4\frac{1}{2} \times 3$ in. Miter the corners of the border.*

3 *Fold another piece of white 8 x 11 in. paper into four so it opens on a long side like a card. Paste your posy and border onto the front quarter of the paper. Open out.*

4 *Using the ivory paper photocopy this 8 x 11 in. sheet 5 times. Fold the pieces of paper into notelets and tie together in a bundle with colorful ribbon.*

*T*his simple gift I wish to be a token of my love for thee.
VICTORIAN VALENTINE

$\mathcal{M}$ANY VICTORIAN women and children took a serious interest in flowers and made comprehensive collections of pressed flowers, leaves and even seaweed. They also used them for craftwork and it was common for specimens to be prettily arranged around hand-written verse. Others were made into charming pictures that were framed and displayed for all to admire. The one shown here is a lavish traditional display of pressed flowers bursting out of a fabulous fern basket.

PRESSED FLOWER PICTURE

MATERIALS

Scissors

Small piece of card

Paintbrush

Rubber-based glue for flowers

Pressed flowers, in differing shapes and sizes; leaves, ferns, grasses, moss and bracken fronds

Tweezers for handling flowers

Toothpicks

Handmade paper to fit frame

10 in. square picture frame

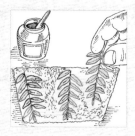

1 Cut a basket shape from the card, paint glue over the surface and stick the moss tightly onto the card. Cut fern leaves and bracken fronds to required length and stick them over the moss to imitate a woven basket.

2 Stick the fern basket onto a piece of handmade paper approximately 7 × 8 in. or to fit a ready-made frame.

3 Lay your flowers, leaves and grasses into the basket in a bouquet arrangement. When you are happy with your design, stick them in place. When the glue is dry, frame the finished picture.

PRESSED FLOWER CARD

$\mathcal{Y}$ou can buy ready-made cards, the front of which is an oval window mount. Suitable flowers for pressing are rosebay willow herb, cranesbill, geranium, potentillas, geums, statice, and cistus.

MATERIALS

Single pressed flower (cistus) and selection of smaller ones

Absorbent paper

Tweezers for handling flowers

Piece of pink paper to fit behind oval window

Ready-made card with oval window mount

Pencil

Rubber-based glue for flowers

Paper glue

Toothpicks for applying the glue

Small scissors

White paper doily

Wire-edged ribbon, color chosen to match flower

1 Pick suitable flowers on a dry day. Carefully lay your specimens onto a folded sheet of absorbent paper. Fold over to enclose the flowers and place between the leaves of a heavy book. It takes about two weeks to press them successfully.

2 Slip the pink paper behind the oval opening of the card and trace the shape of the mount very faintly in pencil onto the backing paper where the flowers will be arranged.

3 Open out the card and arrange your flower design within the pencilled area. Place the large flower centrally and stick it down carefully, dabbing the glue under the flower petals.

4 Glue the small statice flowerheads around the oval facing inwards so that the stems will be hidden by the mount. When you are happy with the design close the card, gluing the backing paper to the back of the oval mount.

5 Cut out small sections of paper doily, then arrange and glue them in position around the oval mount on the front of the card.

6 Cut two slits along the folded side, push the ribbon through and tie into a bow. Trim the ends at an angle.

$\mathcal{W}$hen daisies pied and violets blue, And ladysmocks all silver white, And cuckoo buds of yellow hue, Do paint the meadows with delight.

"Spring," Love's Labour's Lost
WILLIAM SHAKESPEARE
1564–1616

LEAFY LAMPSHADE

DELICATE SKELETONIZED leaves have been used to decorate this pretty lampshade. Use a plain paper shade so that the intricate veining of the leaves shows through to best effect when the lamp is lit. This shade is quick to make and creates an effective home accessory. Skeletonized willow leaves have been used here; they are commercially available from a good florist and are relatively inexpensive.

MATERIALS

Selection of skeletonized willow leaves
Ready-made natural paper lampshade
Paintbrush
Rubber-based glue

1 Collect a variety of undamaged leaves in midsummer. Soak in a bowl of rainwater for about a month; this softens the leaf tissue.

HOW TO SKELETONIZE LEAVES

"**R**eady made" skeletonized leaves are not hard to find; look carefully for them when you walk through woods. If you want a variety of shapes and perfect leaves with a predictable result, however, you need to make them yourself. Fleshy leaves are the best, and magnolia are particularly suitable.

1 Try out the leaves against the lampshade, holding up one or two at a time to plan their positions. When you have decided on your design, brush the back of a leaf very thinly with the glue.

2 Put the leaf in position on the shade. As the leaves will be decorating a curved surface you will need to press each one securely. Continue sticking leaves evenly around the shade, leaving an even gap between each.

2 Take the leaves out of the rainwater and rinse them under cold water.

3 Brush them very gently with a soft brush to remove the cotton tissue from the delicate leaf veins. Allow to dry.

4 Iron them carefully and place them between the pages of a book to store them flat until needed for use.

BEADED GLOVES

*I*T IS STILL possible to find exquisite examples of Victorian beadwork, often used to decorate purses, ladies' jackets, belts, and all manner of accessories. Much patience was required to create the characteristic tightly packed designs and, as in all Victorian needlecrafts, the flower motif was very common. Tiny metal beads and sequins have been used to transform these rich green velour gloves into stunning evening wear.

MATERIALS

Pair of green velour gloves
Tailor's chalk
Selection of tiny metal beads
Needle
Dark green thread
Round, bronze-coloured sequins
Leaf-shaped sequins
4 pink flower sequins

1 Draw your design onto the back of each glove with the tailor's chalk. It is best to keep your design fairly simple.

2 Using some of the metal beads, sew each bead separately onto the glove, making a ring around the center of the flower.

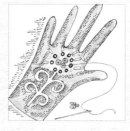

3 Sew the round sequins into the center of the flower.

OPERA

*T*he young Princess Victoria during her austere and lonely childhood was taken to the opera and ballet as often as three times a week, and became infatuated with that exciting, emotional world. In her journal she records her youthful foray into theater criticism. "I was very much amused" is her summing up of an evening in the Royal box or, later, "I was very very much amused," or "I WAS VERY VERY MUCH AMUSED INDEED," underlined three times.

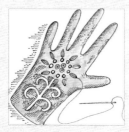

4 Sew the leaf-shaped sequins around this center to form the petals.

5 Sew more tiny metal beads down the stem and along the tendrils.

6 Sew each pink flower sequin under each tendril.

*See! how she leans her cheek
upon her hand:
O! that I were a glove upon that hand,
That I might touch that cheek.*

Romeo and Juliet
WILLIAM SHAKESPEARE
(1564–1616)

PICTURE MOUNT

*T*HIS PRETTY pressed flower picture mount is a lovely way to frame a special photograph and perhaps to remember a favorite garden in the height of summer. Pressed flowers are very fragile and it is more practical to use them to decorate the mount rather than the frame, so that they will be protected under glass.

MATERIALS

Selection of dried flowers and leaves
Ivory card mount (oval-shaped opening)
Rubber-based glue
Toothpicks for applying glue
Tweezers for handling flowers

1 Arrange the pressed flowers and leaves onto the card mount, emphasizing two diagonally opposite corners.

2 When you are happy with your design, starting at the top right-hand corner, dab small amounts of glue onto the card and press the flowers and leaves gently in place.

3 Repeat the process on the lower left-hand corner and allow the glue to dry thoroughly before mounting and framing your picture.

DÉCOUPAGE PICTURE FRAME

*D*ÉCOUPAGE BECAME a fashionable craze in the nineteenth century. The new developments in the printing industry made a greater variety of printed images and scraps available. These were avidly collected and pasted onto all manner of household items, such as frames, boxes, and fire screens.

MATERIALS

Picture frame 9 × 11 in., with
flat front 2¹⁄₂ in. wide

Cream-colored paint

Paintbrush

Scissors

Facsimile Victorian scraps of flowers

Wallpaper paste

Matt polyurethane varnish

Paintbrush for varnish

Sandpaper

1 Paint the frame with two coats of paint and allow to dry thoroughly.

2 Cut out the scraps and arrange them around the frame to help you decide on your final design.

3 Paste the frame and stick the scraps in place with the wallpaper paste. Press them firmly to expel any air bubbles. Allow the frame to dry.

4 Varnish with 3 coats of varnish, sanding the penultimate coat lightly to achieve a smooth finish. You can achieve an antique effect by adding a little burnt umber oil paint to the varnish.

GLASS FLOWERS

*I*T WAS COMMON for Victorian homes to have wonderful arrangements of dried flowers in the living rooms. Garden flowers were picked at the height of the summer season and hung to dry in airy potting sheds. Roses, peonies, lavender, and marigolds dry particularly well and were great favorites. This lovely arrangement is displayed beneath a glass dome, a practical and popular device, much favored in Victorian times for preserving flowers and protecting them from household dust. In the language of flowers this dried arrangement would have signified "Thou art all that is lovely" (rose), shame or bashfulness (peony), and grief (marigold). Perhaps the giver wished to make atonement for a careless remark.

MATERIALS

Cone-shaped oasis foam

Glass dome and stand

Scissors

Paper posy holder or doily

Clippers

Selection of dried flowers including hydrangeas, roses, peonies, lavender and marigolds

*F*lowers or aromatic plants require the smallest increase of heat beyond the temperature of the season, provided that season be genial: something more for rinds or roots and a greater heat for fruits: but this heat must not be carried to excess.

Enquire Within Upon Everything 1894

1 Make sure the oasis cone fits under the dome with enough room to accommodate the flowers. It can be trimmed with a sharp kitchen knife if necessary.

2 Cut the center of a doily or paper posy holder and push it over the oasis cone down to the base.

3 Cut the stems of the flowers to approximately 1¼ in. and start arranging the larger flowers in a circle around the base of the cone.

4 Change the type of flower and the color with each new circle, grading the flower sizes towards the top.

5 *Fill the spaces between the large flowers such as the roses and peonies with tightly packed small bunches of lavender.*

6 *Finish the arrangement by choosing one perfect bud or flower to top the display. Fit the glass dome in place, and make any necessary adjustments to the flowers.*

HOW TO DRY FLOWERS

*I*t is best to pick your chosen flowers on a dry, warm day just before they are in full bloom. This is because the blossoms continue to develop after they are picked and you want the petals to be secure. Strip off most of the leaves and gather them into small bunches of about 5 blooms, tying them loosely with string. Hang them upside down near the ceiling of a warm airy room; an old-fashioned linen closet is ideal. The largest flowers, such as peonies, are best hung singly as they can easily become distorted in a bunch. The flowers are ready for use when they are dry and papery to the touch with brittle stems. Store them in a dust-free environment until ready for use.

*I*t is the watchful eye of the mistress that keeps the home beautiful with the freshness of cleanliness and the calm of repose. Through her vigilance alone will the servants prove faithful in the performance of their duty.

Warne's Model Cookery 1869

BOOKMARK AND GIFT TAGS

BOOKS WERE treasured possessions in the Victorian household. They were often expensive to buy and lavishly bound in gold embossed leather. A small volume of poetry was a common addition to a lady's accessories, and usually enclosed a pretty bookmark, often made by the lady herself.

BOOKMARK

MATERIALS

Pressed flowers (viola and love-in-the-mist (Nigella)) and fern leaves

Tweezers for handling flowers

Ivory card 6¼ × 1½ in.

Rubber cement

Toothpick

Pale blue card 7 × 2 in.

Scissors

Hole punch

12 in. length of tartan ribbon, ¾ in. wide

1 Arrange the flowers centrally over the leaves in a rectangular shape on the prepared card. When you are happy with your design, carefully stick the specimens in place, dabbing the cement on with the toothpick.

2 Stick onto pale blue card, leaving a ¼ in. margin all round. Cut a round tab at the top of the bookmark, then punch a hole in the tab. Thread and knot the ribbon through, then trim the ends at an angle.

GIFT TAGS

*T*hese simple and delicate-looking gift tags, decorated with single specimen flowers and newly formed leaves, will make an enchanting addition to a special present.

MATERIALS

Assorted scraps of recycled paper in pastel shades

Pencil

Scissors

Hole-punch

Pressed specimen flowers (love-in-the-mist (Nigella))

Small new fern leaves

Rubber cement

Toothpick

Matching silk ribbon ½ in. wide

1 Using small household objects as templates such as a matchbox or a lid, draw around it onto the colored paper. Cut the shape out and mount on different-colored paper, leaving a small margin around it. Remember to leave a tab at one end; punch a hole in this.

2 Carefully stick the specimen flowers in place, then decorate with leaves.

3 Attach the silk ribbon through the punched hole and trim the ends.

For, to the noble mind,
Rich gifts wax poor when givers prove unkind.

Hamlet
WILLIAM SHAKESPEARE (1564–1616)

POTPOURRI

THE VICTORIANS delighted in the natural world and were keen gardeners. Herbs and flowers were grown for use in the kitchen and to decorate the house in summer and winter. Pretty bowls of homemade potpourri were distributed throughout the house as an evocative and fragrant reminder of the garden at the height of summer.

ROSE AND LAVENDER POTPOURRI

MATERIALS

Small bowl

1 teaspoon cinnamon powder

1 teaspoon whole cloves

½ teaspoon ground nutmeg

¾ oz. orris root powder

3 drops of lavender essential oil

3 drops of rose essential oil

Large bowl

2½ cups mixed summer flowers, predominantly rose petals, buds and blooms

1¼ cups mixed lemon verbena, eau de Cologne mint, scented geranium leaves

1 oz. lavender

Dried flowers to decorate, including rosebuds, blooms and whole lavender

1 In a small bowl, mix together the spices, orris root powder, and essential oils.

2 Rub the mixture between your fingers, making sure that the oil penetrates the mixture evenly.

3 In a large bowl mix together all the remaining ingredients, remembering to put aside some flowers for the surface decoration.

4 Add the mixture of orris root, spices, and oils to the bowl of dry ingredients. Stir together to produce an evenly scented mixture.

5 Put this mixture into an airtight container and leave in a dark place for 3 weeks, occasionally shaking it. The longer you leave the mixture, the stronger the fragrance will become.

6 Remove the potpourri from the airtight container and put into a pretty china bowl. Decorate the surface with flowers.

❧ SACHETS ❧

*T*hese exquisite little sachets filled with rose
and lavender potpourri will delicately impart
their scent to your linen and simultaneously
help to keep the moths at bay.

MATERIALS

Scraps of printed fabric; cotton lawn or silk are most suitable

Scissors

Needle and matching thread

Potpourri mixture

Pressed flowers of your choice

Fine net

Soft lace or crochet

*The smallest scraps of
lace, ribbon, and pretty
fabrics can be made into
little bags that can then
be lightly stuffed with
highly scented potpourri.
For a really unusual
decoration, lightly glue a
single pressed rosebud or
a group of pressed flowers
to the front of the sachet.
Protect by covering with a
fine net and finish by
adding a soft lace trim.*

*T*he maid of the Countess De Neige
Put others all in a rage.
What gave her such cachet
Were drawers full of sachets
Of lavender, rosemary and sage.

VICTORIAN LIMERICK

CRYSTALLIZED VIOLETS

CRYSTALLIZED VIOLETS surpass any other form of cake decoration and are traditionally used to decorate fine chocolate cakes. They look best arranged in a simple posy or as a circle of alternate leaves and flowers. You need to pick the violets and their heart-shaped leaves on a dry day. Keep them fresh in a jar of water while you are working since they wilt quickly.

MATERIALS

2 egg-whites
Artist's paintbrush
Violet flowers and leaves
4 oz. granulated sugar
Fine sieve
Wax paper
Wire rack

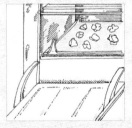

1 Beat the egg-whites until they are white and frothy. With the paintbrush paint each flower carefully with the egg-white. Take care to paint the underside of the petals as well.

2 Holding the flower by its stalk, gently dust with the granulated sugar, using a fine sieve. Turn the flower and dust the underside as well.

3 Lay a sheet of wax paper onto the wire rack, and set the flowers down, making sure they do not touch.

4 Put the rack of flowers to dry in a warm airy place. A linen closet is ideal; alternatively place the rack in a "cool" oven with the door open until the flowers are dry.

5 To store the crystallized flowers, place them between layers of wax paper in an airtight container.

TEAPOT STAND

*T*EA WAS AN important occasion in the Victorian household, especially when guests were expected. The best china was used, along with the silver teapot, and delicious small sandwiches, cakes and fancies were served. The craft of découpage was extremely popular and this elegant teapot stand is an ideal small project to try.

MATERIALS

Round table mat	*Prints of botanical illustrations*	*Rag*
Fine sandpaper	*Small scissors*	*Burnt umber oil paint*
Mauve paint	*Wallpaper paste*	*Polyurethane varnish*
Paintbrush	*Crackle varnish*	*Brush for varnish*

1 Sand the surface of the table mat to provide a key for the paint.

2 Paint with 2 coats of mauve paint.

3 Carefully cut out the botanical illustrations with the small scissors.

4 When you have decided where to lay the prints, apply paste to the mat and stick them down, easing out any trapped air bubbles with your fingers.

5 Allow to dry and apply the crackle glaze following the maker's instructions. The second coat may be dried with a hair dryer.

6 Rub the burnt umber oil paint into the crackles with the rag, then wipe off the excess with a clean rag. Allow the teapot stand to dry and apply at least 5 coats of polyurethane varnish. For a really smooth finish, lightly sand the penultimate coat.

SHELL BOXES

THE VICTORIANS had a passion for collecting shells, and also seaweed, which was pressed and arranged into albums. It is still possible to find stunning examples of "the sailor's Valentine" – framed pictures of exquisite tiny shells arranged into a "shell mosaic." These little boxes with their pearly shell decorations will not fail to grace any dressing table.

He had 42 boxes all carefully packed,
With his name painted clearly on each
But, since he omitted to mention the fact,
They were all left behind on the beach.

The Hunting of the Snark
LEWIS CARROLL 1832–98

MATERIALS

Small wooden boxes – heart-shaped, rectangular or oval

Fine sandpaper

Dusty pink paint

Gilt cream

Rag

White glue

Selection of small shells including petal-shaped shells

Tweezers

Paper lace

1 *Lightly sand the box and its lid with fine sandpaper. Apply 2 coats of paint. Allow to dry.*

2 *Lightly rub the gilt cream over the sides of the box and the edge of the lid. Polish with a clean rag.*

3 *Glue a pearly spiral shell onto the center of the box lid.*

4 *Glue petal-shaped shells around the central shell to make a flower shape.*

You could also try arranging shells as a frame around a pretty Victorian scrap pasted to the lid of a box.

Do not keep the alabaster boxes of your love and tenderness sealed up until your friends are dead. Fill their lives with sweetness. Speak approving cheering words while their hearts can be thrilled by them.

HENRY WARD
BEECHER 1831–87

5 Surround the flower with tightly packed tiny pearly shells. Finish off the design with 2 rows of contrasting shells, following the edge of the lid.

6 Finish by gluing paper lace around the base and bottom edge of the box.

And the hyacinth purple, and white and blue,
Which flung from its bells a sweet peal anew
Of music so delicate, soft and intense,
It was felt like an odour within the sense.

From *Spring Flowers*
PERCY BYSSHE SHELLEY
(1792–1822)

HYACINTHS AND GARLANDS

*W*HO CAN resist the beauty and heady perfume of a hyacinth grown indoors, an early messenger of spring? A variety of spring bulbs were prepared by the gardener to bring into the Victorian house to flower early in the year. Among the most popular, the strongly perfumed hyacinth was grown in specially designed glasses. Later in the year scented garlands, made from flowers fresh from the garden, were used to decorate the home on festive occasions.

GARLAND

*F*or a special occasion drape this lovely scented garland over a picture, fireplace or ornamental mirror frame.

MATERIALS

Ball of string
Assortment of flowers and leaves, according to season
Reel of florists' wire
3 ft. matching wired ribbon.

1 Tie a loop at each end of a piece of string 32 in. long.

2 Make small bunches of leaves and flowers. Lay them onto the string and bind them on with florists' wire. Add more bunches, each one overlapping the previous bunch. Make sure the garland is completely covered, both front and back.

3 Add a ribbon bow at each end, and hang a small bunch of leaves and flowers from behind the bows.

O, Brignal banks are wild and fair,
And Greta woods are green,
And you may gather garlands there
Would grace a summer queen.

Rokeby
SIR WALTER SCOTT (1771–1832)

STENCILLED NOTEBOOK

*T*HE VICTORIANS took an enthusiastic interest in botany, and ferns had a particular appeal to their romantic notions since they grew in wild and exotic places. Keen collectors assembled fern albums, even displaying living examples in specially designed containers. The intricate feathery fronds of the fern create a beautiful design when used as a stencil.

MATERIALS

Notebook with hard cover

Newspaper

Spray paint – bright green, dark green and brown

Pressed ferns

Scissors

Burnt umber oil paint

Polyurethane varnish

Brush

Fine sandpaper

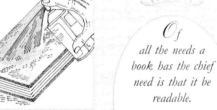

1 Place the book on newspaper and spray the front and back with the bright green paint.

2 When the paint has dried, spray over very lightly with darker green paint to give a mottled effect.

*O*f
all the needs a book has the chief need is that it be readable.

Autobiography
ANTHONY
TROLLOPE
(1815–82

3 Cut the fern specimens to fit the size of the book and lay them onto the cover quite flat. Spray carefully with the brown paint, just going over the edges slightly to create an outline.

4 Remove the ferns and repeat on the back of the book.

5 Mix a small amount of burnt umber oil into some varnish, and apply 3 coats, or more if the cover of the book is at all absorbent. Sand the penultimate coat lightly to achieve a smooth finish.

A birdie with a yellow bill
Hopped upon the window-sill,
Cocked his shining eye and said,
"Ain't you 'shamed you sleepy head?"

Time to Rise
ROBERT LOUIS STEVENSON
(1850–94)

HERB PILLOW

*T*HE VICTORIANS had an extensive knowledge of the therapeutic uses of fragrant herbs and flowers. Advice abounded on the importance of the bedroom arrangements, which had to be spacious, lofty, well-ventilated and uninhabited during the day, and many ills were blamed on the lack of a sound night's sleep. Fresh flowers or potted plants were never placed in a bedroom as they were thought to be injurious to the health at night. This pretty pillow stuffed with sleep-inducing herbs will sweeten the night air.

MATERIALS

20 in. calico

Needle

Thread

Pins

4 cups mixed lime blossom, hops and jasmine flowers

20 in. printed Victorian pattern cotton

3 ft. matching fringed braid

*T*o make a Victorian bed was neither a short nor a simple task. There were usually three mattresses. The heavy bottom mattress, stuffed with straw, was turned only once a week; the middle mattress, made of wool or horsehair, was turned daily; and the feather mattress on top had to be shaken, pummelled, smacked and turned every day until it was as light and puffed as a soufflé.

Life Below Stairs
FRANK E. HUGGETT

1 Cut two pieces of calico 9 × 11 in. Sew up three sides to make a bag and turn inside out.

2 Mix the herbs together and lightly stuff them into the bag.

3 Neatly sew up the open end, and roughly tack across the bag to keep the herbs in place.

4 Cut two pieces of printed fabric. With right sides together sew around three sides, then turn the right way round.

5 Push the calico pillow inside the cotton case, and sew up the open end.

6 Sew matching braid around the edge of the pillow, making sure the braid lies flat around the corners. Finish off neatly.

DRIED FLOWERS

꧁ ✤ ꧂

*T*HE WELL-PLANNED Victorian kitchen garden included beds of flowers grown specifically for cutting. These were used for fresh flower arrangements during the summer for the parlor and dining room. Bunches were hung up to dry in airy potting sheds, kitchens or attics for use in dried-flower displays, the making of fragrant potpourris, scented sachets and therapeutic herb pillows. Most garden flowers are suitable for drying and will keep their color well if the correct procedure is followed.

1 Pick the flowers on a dry, warm day. Select flowers that are freshly opened or still in bud. Lay them carefully in a garden tray.

2 Remove some of the leaves from the stems to encourage quicker drying. Pick the thorns off the rose stems to protect your fingers later on.

3 Put approximately 8 stems together in a loose bunch. Try to keep the flowerheads as loose as possible.

4 Tie the bunches together with gardener's twine and suspend from a line stretched across a room.

TO DRY FLOWERS IN SILICA GEL

*U*SE SILICA GEL to dry special flowers singly. It is a magical process. The crystals have a powerful dessicating effect and so you can dry flowers in a very short time. It has the advantage of preserving the color and form of the bloom perfectly.

*F*lowers particularly suitable for drying are larkspur, roses, achillea, African marigolds, cornflowers, delphiniums, lavender, meadowsweet, astilbes, grasses, love-in-the-mist, and honesty.

MATERIALS

4¹⁄₂ lb. silica gel

Deep-sided baking tray

Flowerheads – roses, pansies, peonies etc.

Aluminum foil to cover tray

1 Put a layer of silica gel in the bottom of the baking tray. Take care not to breathe in the dust of the silica gel.

2 Lay the flowers carefully into the silica and gently sift more gel over the flowerheads to fill in the spaces between the petals.

3 Continue building up layers of flowers and silica gel. Cover with foil and leave for up to a week. Store the silica gel in an airtight container and wash your hands after use.

4 Remove the flowers carefully from the silica gel. They will be perfectly dried in form and color and can be used to stunning effect in floral arrangements.

*I*N THE Victorian home an impressive variety of
toiletries and remedies in the form of perfumes, flower
waters, pomanders, bath oils, and tonics were prepared by
the housekeeper with the assistance of the still-room maid.
Fresh ingredients were provided by the head gardener from
a well-stocked garden.

ORANGE FLOWER WATER TONIC

*T*his tonic makes a refreshing treatment for tired and aging skin, as it stimulates the growth of healthy new cells.

INGREDIENTS

¾ cup orange flower water

½ cup witchhazel

5 drops of glycerin

5 drops of neroli essential oil

Lidded glass jar or bottle

Photocopies of small black and white engravings

Ribbons in associated pastel shades

1 Put all the ingredients into the lidded jar or bottle, and shake vigorously to blend together.

2 Decant into pretty bottles with airtight stoppers.

*O*range blossom is, as we all know, a lucky flower at a wedding. Some say it will ensure the union will be blessed with the patter of tiny feet.

Old English Omen

3 Cut out the black and white photocopies into little labels and attach to the bottles with ribbons tied into decorative bows.

ROSE AND GLYCERIN CLEANSING CREAM

*T*he gentle soothing qualities of this rose-scented cleansing cream make it ideal for removing the dirt and make-up of a busy day.

INGREDIENTS

Double saucepan

3 tablespoons almond oil

4 teaspoons glycerin

2½ tablespoons lanolin

2½ tablespoons beeswax

Glass fireproof basin

Small saucepan

Balloon whisk

Large pinch of borax

4 tablespoons rosewater

1 teaspoon zinc oxide cream

7 drops of rose essential oil

*L*ove is a secret like a bird in a shell like a rose ere it blossom All unseen will it dwell.

JOHN CLARE
1793–1864

1 In a double saucepan slowly heat the almond oil and glycerin together. Put the lanolin and beeswax into the glass basin over a pan of hot water. Mix together. Pour the oil and glycerin mixture into this and beat with the balloon whisk.

2 Dissolve a large pinch of borax in slightly heated rosewater. Add to the lanolin, wax, and oil mixture, beating all the time to achieve a cream-like consistency. Allow to cool.

3 When cool finally beat in the zinc oxide cream and the rose oil. Spoon into pretty jars and label.

POTPOURRI

NOTHING IS more evocative of a garden
in high summer than a pretty bowl of richly
scented potpourri displayed in every room. For
Victorian women, already so industrious
and inventive with other flower crafts,
the collection, drying and
preparation of flowers and herbs
for a variety of recipes was an
enjoyable and practical pastime.

TRADITIONAL VICTORIAN POT-POURRI

INGREDIENTS

1 teaspoon allspice

1 oz. orris root

2 drops of rose oil

2 drops of lavender oil

3 drops of cottage garden mixture oil

5 cups mixed garden flowers – chamomile, rosebuds and petals, larkspur, honeysuckle, marigold, hydrangea

2½ oz. mixed sweet herbs – sweet-cicely, lemon verbena, scented geranium leaves

¾ oz. lavender

Handful of lavender heads to decorate

1 cinnamon stick

1 tablespoon whole cloves

*O*nce you have some experience of making potpourris, try inventing your own recipes using flowers from different seasons. Create a freshly scented bowl of spring flowers with fragrant lily of the valley for a pretty bedroom, or a richly spiced and opulent winter potpourri for a Christmas display. Change the color combinations to suit your room decoration.

1 In a small bowl mix together the allspice, orris root, and essential oils (rose, lavender, and cottage garden).

2 Rub the mixture between your fingers, making sure that the oil penetrates the mixture evenly.

3 Mix together all the remaining ingredients in a large bowl. Break the cinnamon stick into small pieces. Remember to put aside some rosebuds, petals, lavender heads and hydrangea to decorate the finished potpourri.

4 Add the mixture of fixative (the orris root, spices, and oils) to the bowl of dry ingredients. Stir together to produce an evenly scented mixture.

5 Put the mixture in an airtight container and store in a dark place for three weeks, occasionally shaking the container. The longer you leave the mixture, the stronger the fragrance will become. Eventually remove from the container and display in a beautiful blue and white china bowl.

*Two hairs on your shoulder
are better than one,
As two means a letter, and one means none.*

Old English Proverb

HAIR TOILETRIES

❧

*I*N THE nineteenth century women took pride in styling their hair beautifully, grooming it with typical Victorian attention to detail. With the help of a lady's maid it was washed, conditioned, scented and strengthened with all manner of preparations. These were expertly concocted by the housekeeper from a combination of natural ingredients picked from the garden by the head gardener and more unusual products that were widely available from the local pharmacy. Rosemary, an aromatic sun-loving herb, is easy to grow and popularly cultivated in many gardens; it is a natural conditioner and an ideal herb for hair care.

ROSEMARY SHAMPOO

*T*he addition of fresh rosemary to this gentle shampoo helps to condition and strengthen hair. It has been used throughout the ages as a well-tried herb for stimulating hair growth.

INGREDIENTS

1 bunch of fresh rosemary

1¼ cups of distilled water

small bottle unscented shampoo (baby shampoo is ideal)

4 drops of rosemary essential oil

2 Strain the rosemary decoction into a large screw-topped jar, add the unscented shampoo and 4 drops of essential oil, then shake well to mix.

1 Put the fresh rosemary in a saucepan with the distilled water. Bring to the boil and simmer for half an hour, reducing the amount of liquid by half to ¾ cup. Allow to cool.

3 Decant into pretty bottles.

ROSEMARY AND LAVENDER HAIR MASSAGE OIL

*N*ourish your hair and add luster to it with this fragrant oil. To use the oil, warm it slightly, then massage it into the hair vigorously with your fingers. Comb it out and leave for 30 minutes. Wash off with rosemary shampoo.

INGREDIENTS

½ cup almond oil

3 drops of rosemary essential oil

3 drops of lavender essential oil

A rosemary bush will mature and grow old, Only where a woman heads the household.

Old English Proverb

1 In a small jug, mix the almond oil with the essential oils.

2 Decant into pretty bottles.

SCENTED CANDLES

———❦———

Wax candles were expensive and used sparingly in all but the grandest houses. The ordinary household made do with the failing light of evening for as long as possible. It was not uncommon for wax and tallow candles to be made by the ever-industrious housekeeper. The best candles were brought out for special occasions or when guests were expected. These unusual scented floating candles arranged among fresh flowerheads make an elegant centerpiece to a table setting.

MATERIALS

1 lb. paraffin wax

Double saucepan

Wax dye disks in pink and orange

Wax perfume or essential oils – rose and gardenia

Tin miniature tart cases in assorted sizes

18 in. primed wick

A number of flat-headed flowers – roses, marigolds or gardenias

1 Put the paraffin wax into the double saucepan. Heat the water in the bottom pan and the wax will slowly melt.

2 Add a small piece of the wax dye disk to color the wax; the more dye, the deeper the color.

3 Add a few drops of wax perfume or essential oil.

4 Pour the melted wax carefully into the molds and allow to set slightly.

5 Cut the wick into 2 in. lengths and push each piece into the center of the setting wax. As the wax begins to harden, it will shrink a little. It may be necessary to "top up" the candle with a little more molten wax.

6 Release the candles from the molds and intersperse with flat-headed flowers in an elegant dish filled with water.

TO THE WIFE WHO HAS TO PROVIDE ON VERY SLENDER MEANS

———

Take care that your table-linen is spotlessly pure and white, the cloth well pressed, that you have table napkins and finger glasses for dessert. These little elegancies cost next to nothing and add immensely to the air of comfort and refinement which your table should possess. In summer, manage if possible to have a centre ornament of candles and flowers, if only a cheap vase.

Warnes Model Cookery and Housekeeping 1869

The fairest things have fleetest end,
Their scent survives their close:
But the rose's scent is bitterness
To him that loved the rose.

DAISY FRANCIS THOMPSON
1859–1907

BATH OILS

*D*URING THE nineteenth century there were great developments in plumbing and sanitation, and permanently installed baths became more common. The strenuous task of filling the baths with hot water was allotted to the servants of the house. The Victorians believed that taking regular baths braced the body and enlivened the spirit, promoting health, cleanliness, and free circulation of the blood.

PENNYROYAL BATH VINEGAR

A refreshing and antiseptic bath preparation. Use one cupful per bath.

INGREDIENTS

1¼ cups cider vinegar
1¼ cups water
One handful of pennyroyal
One handful of lemon balm

1 Bring the vinegar and water to the boil in a large saucepan.

2 Add the herbs, remove the pan from the heat and cover with a lid. Leave to steep overnight.

3 Strain the infusion into a screw-topped jar. Shake well and decant into decorative bottles. Use within one or two weeks.

NEROLI AND CHAMOMILE SCENTED BUBBLE BATH

*N*eroli essential oil, extracted from fragrant orange blossoms, is well known for its healing qualities; it is the main ingredient in this soothing bubble bath.

1 Add 10 drops of neroli and 5 drops of chamomile essential oil to ¾ cup of unscented mild baby bath liquid.

2 Pour under the hot tap when the bath is running and relax in the soothing fragrance.

O *Beauty, passing beauty! sweetest Sweet!*
How can'st thou let me waste my youth in sighs?
I only ask to sit beside thy feet.
Thou knowest I dare not look into thine eyes.

Poems
ALFRED, LORD TENNYSON 1809–92

A TRADITIONAL HERBAL FOOT BATH

*T*his is an effective therapeutic treatment to soothe and refresh aching feet.

1 Add a generous handful of lavender and spearmint with a handful of sea salt to a large bowl of water.

2 Immerse the feet in this for at least 10 minutes and your whole being will feel revived.

If you could see my legs when I take my boots off, you'd form some idea of what unrequited affection is.

Mr Toots
Dombey and Son
CHARLES DICKENS
1812–70

REJUVENATING BATH OIL

*S*prinkle a few drops of this fragrant oil into your bath after a tiring day.

1 To ¾ cup of base dispersing oil add 5 drops each of lavender, rosemary, and juniper essential oil.

2 Store in pretty bottles and add a small quantity to your bath to revitalize you.

GARDENER'S HAND CREAM

ONE OF the worst hazards facing the enthusiastic gardener who does not like wearing gloves is rough, dry hands. Since garden soil dries the skin it is essential to have a good soothing cream to restore, soften and nourish the vulnerable skin on your hands. For this recipe it is necessary to make an infusion of elderflowers. Put two handfuls of fresh elderflowers into a saucepan. (Dried elderflowers may be used if fresh are not available.) Pour over 2½ cups of boiled distilled water. Cover and allow to steep for one hour. Strain into jars and store in the refrigerator.

CALENDULA AND ELDERFLOWER HAND CREAM

INGREDIENTS

Bain-marie

4 teaspoons beeswax

4 teaspoons lanolin

4 teaspoons cocoa butter

4½ teaspoons calendula oil

1¼ teaspoon glycerin

Large pinch of borax

2½ tablespoons elderflower infusion

Small jug

5 drops of melissa essential oil

*I'm a broken hearted
gardener, and don't know what to do,
My love she is inconsistent, and a fickle jade too,
One smile from her lips will never be forgot,
It refreshes like a smile from a watering pot.*

Victorian Street Ballad

1 In the bain-marie gently melt the beeswax and stir in the lanolin and cocoa butter.

2 Add the warmed calendula oil and glycerin to the melted lanolin, cocoa butter, and beeswax mixture.

3 Dissolve the borax in the warmed elderflower infusion in a jug and then add to the mixture. Continue stirring until it thickens. This will occur as the mixture cools.

4 Add the drops of melissa oil. Stir the mixture and spoon into jars.

ROSE AND VIOLET

*V*ICTORIAN LADIES were passionate about flowers. They studied botany in childhood and set about assembling stunning collections of pressed flowers, arranging them delightfully in beautifully bound albums. Flowers became all-pervasive in designs for all manner of items. Communication through symbolism, aided by the many editions of the popular little book, *The Language of Flowers*, became a common means of expression.

PRESSED VIOLET GREETINGS CARD

MATERIALS

Handmade natural paper 4¹/₂ × 7 in.

Pressed violet with leaves

Rubber cement for plant material

Toothpicks for applying glue

20 in. paper lace ribbon

Paper glue

Small scissors

20 in. faded violet satin ribbon ¹/₂ in. wide

PRESSED FLOWERS

*I*t takes about two weeks to press flowers successfully. If you do not have a flower press, just lay your specimens carefully between absorbent paper within the pages of a heavy book.

---

1 Fold the paper neatly in half lengthways to make a stand-up card.

2 Carefully place the pressed violet in position on the front of the card, then remove and place little dabs of rubber glue with the toothpick on the card where the violet leaves and stalk will appear. Press the flower in place and allow the glue to dry.

3 Cut the paper lace ribbon to trim the outside edges of the card. Glue in place with paper glue.

4 Finally, make two slits along the fold of the card, thread the satin ribbon through and tie into a pretty bow. You may also like to write the botanical name beneath the pressed flower.

---

*T*he Victorians excelled in the domestic production of fragrant floral waters, and most households produced the well-known favorites of lavender, rose and violet. Floral waters and essential oils are widely available today and it is surprisingly simple to make lovely naturally scented perfumes with them.

ROSE AND VIOLET PERFUME

INGREDIENTS

¹/₂ cup rosewater

5 tablespoons violet toilet water (or, if this is difficult to obtain, 10 drops of Devonshire violet perfume mixed with 2 tablespoons eau de Cologne)

10 drops of rose essential oil

¹/₂ cup vodka

1 Mix all the ingredients together in a china jug.

2 Decant into pretty glass perfume bottles with glass stoppers.

HERB OIL AND VINEGAR

DURING THE nineteenth century recipe books abounded with advice on the varied uses of herbs both in the kitchen and the sick-room, and to this day they are eaten for their flavor and are widely used for medicinal purposes. These decorative molded glass bottles filled with herb-flavored oil and vinegar would look attractive on your kitchen shelves. Simple to produce, with their decorative sealed corks they would also make a special gift for an enthusiastic cook.

❧ ROSEMARY OIL ❧

INGREDIENTS

Basin

Fresh rosemary

5 cups olive oil

Muslin

Molded glass bottle with cork

Sealing wax

Blue ribbon

1 Loosely fill a basin with 2 handfuls of freshly gathered rosemary.

2 Pour 5 cups of good olive oil over the fresh herbs. Cover with muslin and put in a warm airy place; a sunny windowsill is ideal. Allow to steep for two weeks and stir daily.

3 Strain through muslin and decant into a molded glass bottle in which you have previously inserted a sprig of fresh rosemary.

4 Place the cork in the top of the bottle. Seal with a coin on the hot sealing wax. Cut a length of ribbon and place around the neck of the bottle, drip sealing wax onto the place where the ribbons cross on the front of the bottle, then make an impression with the coin.

HOW TO SEAL

1 Drip the lighted sealing wax onto the tops and sides of the cork.

2 While the wax is still soft, press a coin onto the top of the cork to make an impression.

❧ TARRAGON VINEGAR ❧

INGREDIENTS

Fresh tarragon

1 quart screw-topped jar

5 cups cider vinegar

Muslin

Molded glass bottle with cork

Sealing wax

Ribbon

1 Pick 2 handfuls of fresh tarragon and pack loosely into a quart screw-topped glass jar.

2 Heat 5 cups of cider vinegar, making sure it does not boil, and pour over the fresh herbs. Screw on the lid and place the jar in a warm dry place. Shake the jar every day for two weeks.

3 Strain the liquid through muslin and decant into a molded glass bottle to match the herb oil. Push a sprig of fresh tarragon into the bottle.

4 Cork the bottle and seal with sealing wax, making an impression with a coin into the hot wax on the top of the cork. Cut a length of ribbon and place around the neck of the bottle, drip sealing wax onto the place where the ribbons cross and seal with a coin.

The use of vinegar
is recommended when
an overdose of strong
wine, spirit, opium, or
other narcotic poisoning
has been taken.

The Complete Servant
SAMUEL AND SARAH
ADAMS 1825

OVEN GLOVES

NTIL THE middle of the nineteenth century when more sophisticated kitchen ranges began to be installed with a cast-iron oven on one side and a boiler heater on the other, most of the cooking was done over an open fire. There was a strict hierarchy in the kitchen. It was the cook who planned and prepared the meals and supervised the pantries and storerooms. The scullery maid's job was to black-lead and light the kitchen range early in the morning in preparation for the hard work of the day. These practical oven gloves will add an atmosphere of nostalgia to the most modern of kitchens; they have lemon balm and cloves sewn into the padding, so they release their scent when warm.

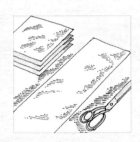

1 Cut one length of cotton interlining 32 × 7 in. Cut four pieces 7 in. square.

MATERIALS

20 in. cotton interlining	Large handful of lemon balm
Scissors	16 in. woven light upholstery fabric
Needle and thread	8 ft. bias binding in matching color
Large handful of whole cloves	8 ft. cotton fringed braid

2 Make two pockets with the four pieces of cotton interlining by sewing up three sides. Fill loosely with whole cloves and lemon balm leaves. Tack loosely across the "pockets" to hold the spices in place. Close the open side.

3 Lay these herb and spice-filled pockets onto either end of the longer strip. Tack in place.

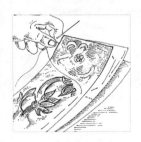

4 Cut two lengths of the upholstery fabric 7 × 32 in. Place the cotton interlining with spice-filled pockets between these two lengths; tack in place.

5 Cut two lengths of fabric 7 in. square and, with reverse side showing, bind one edge with bias binding, lay onto each end of the gloves, and tack in place, leaving bound edge free for hands to go in.

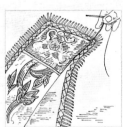

6 Bind around the perimeter of the gloves with the rest of the bias binding. For a special touch, sew cotton fringe around the gloves.

MILK BATH

*T*HE CUSTOM of scenting baths goes back to Roman times when handfuls of fresh lavender were thrown into bath water both to perfume and disinfect. Bathing can be a luxurious experience – Cleopatra is famous for having bathed in asses' milk, surely the ultimate luxury aid for softening and conditioning the skin. In the recipe given here spicily scented fennel acts as a stimulant, while marigold has well-known healing properties.

MARIGOLD AND FENNEL MILK BATH

MATERIALS

10 in. butter muslin

10 tablespoons whole milk powder

4 oz. dried fennel seeds

2 oz. dried marigold flowers

Narrow ribbon in assorted colors

*T*he marigold flower like bright little sunbursts scattered about the garden possesses healing qualities that greatly exceed its humble appearance.

1 Cut out a circle of muslin roughly 10 in. in diameter. For ease, draw around an upturned plate.

2 In a bowl mix together the whole milk powder, fennel seeds, and marigold flowers.

3 Put a large handful of the mixture into the center of the muslin circle. Gather up the edges to form a pouch shape. Tie tightly at the top with the ribbon, adding a long loop if you wish to hang the milk bath beneath the hot tap.

ORANGE SACHETS

*T*HESE CHARMING little fragrant sachets are prettily edged in lace and loosely filled with spicy orange peel and dried chamomile, perhaps gathered from the edges of a field. They will subtly impart their gentle perfume to your freshly laundered table linen.

ORANGE PEEL AND CHAMOMILE SACHETS

MATERIALS

2 oz. dried chamomile flowerheads

4 oz. dried orange peel

Small basin

Scissors

2 lengths of 8 in. Victorian print cotton lawn

Needle and matching thread

Variety of lace for edging

Assorted ribbons for decorative bows

1 Put the chamomile and orange peel into a small basin and mix together thoroughly. Cut two identical pieces of cotton material in each of a square and diamond shape, no more than 4 in. wide.

2 Turn the right sides together and hand or machine stitch around the edge. Leave a 1½ in. gap. Turn the sachets the right way round and loosely stuff them with the mixture of flowers and peel.

3 Close the gap neatly and sew the lace around the sachets by hand. Take care at the corners, making sure the lace lies flat. For the finishing touch, sew on pretty little tightly tied bows in complementary colors.

WINTER WREATH

A TRADITIONAL winter wreath made from glossy bay leaves and dried citrus fruits will add a festive note to your winter celebrations.

MATERIALS

Large bunch of small sprays of bay

Smaller bunch of rosemary or curry herb

Reel of fine florists' wire

Clippers

Wire ring

Dried orange rings

Natural raffia

Drink to me only with thine eyes
And I will pledge with mine
Or leave a kiss but in the cup
And I'll not look for wine …
… I sent thee late a rosy wreath
Not so much honouring thee
As giving it a hope that there
It could not wither'd be;

BEN JONSON 1574–1637

1 Gather the bay and rosemary or curry herb into little bunches and bind together with florists' wire. Trim the stems with clippers.

2 Place the bunches, all facing the same way, overlapping each other onto the wire ring. Bind with florists' wire to secure.

3 Continue adding the bunches until the whole ring is covered. Thread some citrus fruit onto a length of natural raffia and tie onto the wreath at intervals with the raffia, leaving an untidy bow to show at the front.

Ill-fitting gas pipes through-out the house supplying the hot-water geyser and gas lamps left a pervasive, much hated, smell. Wreaths of scented greenery and fruits were used at Christmas time to be both decorative and pleasantly odorous.

CECILIA CAVENDISH

SCENTED GARLAND

FOR A SPECIAL occasion, drape this gracious summer scented garland over a fireplace or ornate mirror frame.

MATERIALS

Ball of string

Assortment of summer flowers, such as jasmine (dried or fresh) and bay leaves

Reel of fine florists' wire

3 ft. wired ribbon

1 Tie a loop at one end of the string, which has been cut to the required length.

2 Lay a small bunch of mixed flowers and leaves onto the string and bind tightly with fine florists' wire to secure.

3 Continue adding more small bunches, each one overlapping. Make sure the garland is completely covered with flowers, front and back.

4 When the garland is the required length, secure the wire. Make another loop of string for hanging the garland.

5 Finish by adding a wired ribbon bow, attaching it by wire at both ends.

When daisies pied and violets blue, And lady smocks all silver white, And cuckoo buds of yellow hue, Do paint the meadows with delight.

"Spring", Love's Labour's Lost
WILLIAM SHAKESPEARE
1564–1616

SPARKLING ELDERFLOWER

*A*lthough the butler of the house was responsible for the wine cellar, it was the housekeeper who made the English wines, cordials and syrups, with locally grown ingredients. Here is a recipe for a sparkling elderflower drink that is perfect for summer parties.

INGREDIENTS

6 large heads of elderflowers

Large plastic bucket or similar container

2 lemons

2 lb. white sugar

¼ cup white wine vinegar

11 pints water

Fine sieve

Large pitcher

Six 2½ pint bottles

1 Pick the large heads of elderflowers on a dry day, when they are in full bloom.

2 In a large container put the flowerheads and the juice of 2 lemons, plus the pared rind (discard the bitter white pith). Add the sugar and vinegar, and stir.

3 Add 11 pt. of cold water and leave for 24 hours. Stir occasionally.

4 Strain the liquid through a fine sieve into a large pitcher.

5 Decant into strong bottles. Push the cork well in, and leave for 14 days. After two weeks, the drink will be sparkling and ready to enjoy.

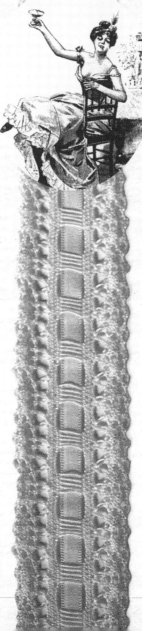

ELDERFLOWER CORDIAL

*E*lderflowers and elderberries, cowslips and gooseberries were just a few of the favorite ingredients for home-made drinks. Dilute this cordial for a refreshing summer drink or pour over freshly picked strawberries.

INGREDIENTS

1 lb. freshly picked elderflowers

2 cups white sugar

2 cups water

Large plastic bucket

Clean cloth (tea towel)

Saucepan

Fine sieve

Pitcher

Sterilized bottle with screw top

1 Gather elderflowers on a dry sunny day. It is said to be best to pick them in the early morning.

2 Boil up the sugar and water until the sugar has dissolved.

3 Pour this syrup over the flowers in the bucket. Mix well, cover with a clean cloth and leave for 24 hours.

4 Put this mixture into the saucepan and simmer for 15 minutes.

5 Remove the elderflowers, squeeze out the syrup and bring to the boil. Then turn the heat down and simmer the liquid for 10 minutes. Allow to cool slightly.

6 Strain the liquid through a fine sieve into a clean pitcher. Pour into a hot sterilized bottle, right up to the top, leaving no air space. Screw the lid on tightly. This cordial needs to be stored in the refrigerator and consumed within a month.

There were numerous methods available to the Victorian housewife of preserving succulent summer fruits, so that they could be enjoyed during the winter months. This luxurious and intoxicating dessert is a traditional Swiss recipe that involves no cooking. Mainly stone fruits are layered with sugar and covered with rum in an earthenware container. When the dessert is ready the fruit will be well impregnated with the rum and surrounded by a delicious dark alcoholic syrup. Fruit can be added throughout the harvest season and this wonderful dish may be enjoyed at its best at Christmas.

TO MAKE EGG NOG

*T*his rich and nourishing drink was traditionally given to invalids. A real old favorite, serve it as a warming winter treat around a blazing log fire.

INGREDIENTS

Yolk of 1 large egg

2 tablespoons honey

1 pint basin

Small glass of brandy

1¹⁄₄ cup double cream

1¹⁄₄ cup milk

Saucepan

1 Beat the egg yolk and honey together in the basin, until it becomes foamy.

2 Stir in the brandy.

3 Mix the cream and milk in the saucepan and bring to boiling point.

4 Pour the cream and milk over the previously mixed ingredients. Stir very well.

5 Pour into glasses or mugs and serve immediately.

❧ TO MAKE RHUMTOPF ❧

INGREDIENTS

Selection of stone fruits as they come into season — cherries, peaches, apricots, and raspberries

Large earthenware crock

13 oz. white granulated sugar to every 17¹⁄₂ oz. of fruit

5 cups white rum

1 With the exception of the raspberries, wash the fruit and pat dry with a tea towel.

2 Put a layer of one kind of fruit at the bottom of the earthenware crock.

*C*hook chook, chook chook, chicken, Lay a little egg for me. I haven't had one since Easter, And now it's half past three, So chook chook, chook chook, chicken Lay a little egg for me.

POPULAR SONG
c. 1900

3 Cover with an equal weight of sugar and pour white rum over this.

4 Continue to build up alternate layers of fruit, sugar and enough rum to cover the fruit completely. Cover with a plate and leave for at least two months.

*T*here was an old man of Thermopylae, Who never did anything properly; But they said, 'If you choose To boil eggs in your shoes, You shall never remain in Thermopylae.'

EDWARD LEAR 1812–88

HOT PUNCH

HOT PUNCH is always a welcome drink on a cold night, and traditionally served after carol singing at Christmas. There is something very comforting about a spiced and sweetened wine fortified with brandy. Victorian household advice and recipe books abound with numerous variations on the ingredients of punch, which played an important part in the social activity of entertaining.

INGREDIENTS

1¼ cups water

Pared rind and juice of 2 lemons

Pared rind and juice of 2 oranges

Cinnamon stick

Large pinch of nutmeg

1 teaspoon of allspice

10 whole cloves

2½ cups granulated sugar

Saucepan

5 cups red wine

1¼ cups brandy

SUMMER VARIATION

A variation to this recipe can be served as sangría, a cool summer party drink. Slice and de-seed two lemons and two oranges, then core and slice two apples. Stir in brandy, wine and lemonade. Add sprigs of lemon balm and serve in jugs with borage flower ice cubes.

1 Put the water, juice and pared rind of lemons and oranges, spices and sugar into a saucepan.

2 Bring slowly to the boil, stir to dissolve the sugar, then simmer for 10 minutes.

3 Strain the liquid, return to the pan, and add the wine and brandy. Reheat, but do not allow the liquid to boil.

4 Pour into a large bowl, add 5 slices of orange and serve hot in small mugs or glasses.

ROSE PETAL JAM

VICTORIAN HOUSEHOLDS had a pantry or store-room amply stacked with homemade jams, syrups, pickles, preserves, and bottled fruit. The rose was a favorite flower, and its delicious perfume was used to scent rosewater, Turkish delight, wines, syrups, perfumes, and potions. Rose petal jam is still widely eaten in the Middle East.

INGREDIENTS

2 lb. cooking apples	Jelly bag or muslin
1 lb. rose petals	4⅓ cups sugar
Large saucepan	2½ tablespoons rose water
Juice of 1 lemon, 1 orange	1 lb. jam jars

1 *Wash but do not peel the apples, then cut them into chunks.*

2 *Cut the bitter white "heel" from each rose petal.*

3 *Put the apples and half the petals into a large saucepan, add water to cover and cook over a medium heat until the apple is tender. Stir in the lemon and orange juice.*

4 *Strain the fruit through a jelly bag or muslin (do not squeeze), until all the liquid is through.*

5 *Add the sugar, the remaining rose petals and rose water. Bring to the boil, stirring constantly. Test the jam by dropping a small spoonful onto a plate and seeing if it cools to a thick jelly. Spoon into sterilized jars. Seal, cut out rings of fabric and tie over the jar lids with a ribbon when cool.*

LABELS

The labels used here were made by photocopying and enlarging old cartouche designs from a source book of copyright-free designs. They were carefully cut out and pasted onto the jars. The labels can be enhanced by writing the names of the jam in a Victorian copperplate style.

LAVENDER FURNITURE POLISH

*L*AVENDER, with its distinctive pungent fragrance, has long been used in the home. To make this lavender-scented furniture polish you first need to make an infusion of lavender. Pour 2 cups of boiling distilled water over two handfuls of fresh lavender. Leave to steep for one hour, then strain and keep in the refrigerator for no longer than four or five days before using.

INGREDIENTS

¾ cup turpentine

1¼ oz. beeswax

⅔ cup strong infusion of lavender

¼ oz. grated soap (olive oil based)

Lavender essential oil

1 Put the turpentine and grated beeswax into a lidded glass jar. Leave for a few days to allow the wax to dissolve. This can be done over a flameless heat, but take care as turpentine is very inflammable!

2 Put the lavender infusion in a small pan, bring it to the boil and stir in the grated soap until it has all melted. Allow to cool.

3 Blend the two mixtures together. Stir vigorously until it has the consistency of double cream.

CRAFTSMEN

*C*rafts guilds were established during the nineteenth century. These ensured that a "man with a trade" would have been an apprentice for at least five years, starting when he was aged twelve or fourteen, and could be relied upon to be knowledgeable and experienced. A skilled craftsman could expect to be paid ten times as much as his un-skilled workmates. Although his occupation prevented him from entering the social circles of the middle classes, he could enjoy many of the trappings of their lifestyle. At the beginning of the twentieth century the status of a master craftsman was similar to that of an average architect.

4 Add 5 drops of lavender essential oil and stir.

5 Pour into bottles or jars ready for use.

SLIPPER BAG

VICTORIAN LADIES had servants who took great pride in keeping their mistress's clothes beautifully laundered. Items of clothing were packed with great care and skill in preparation for a journey. Shoes and slippers often decorated with bows, jewels, clasps, ribbons or laces were placed in their own bag so as not to snag or soil items of fine clothing in the suitcase, trunk or portmanteau.

MATERIALS

Blue damask 12 × 30 in.
White and pale blue thread
3¼ ft. of twisted satin cord with tassels attached
6½ ft. white ric rac
24 in. of white double-edged broderie anglaise
3¼ ft. of white satin woven ribbon

1 *Fold the damask halfway across the length, then tack and machine stitch up both sides.*

2 *Open the stitching on one side at the top. Turn 2½ in. of fabric over the cord to make a hem, turning under ½ in. Pin and tack.*

3 *Turn the bag right side out. Tack and then machine stitch ric rac along the hem line. Knot the two ends of the cord together to create a drawstring top.*

CORONATION SLIPPERS

Queen Victoria's coronation slippers were of a ballet type, embroidered with rose buds and the royal arms in gold. They were lined in white satin reading "All Hail Victoria" in a wreath of shamrock, thistle, and roses.

4 *From the inside, stitch the broderie anglaise one-third down onto the top of the bag. Turn the other two-thirds back to make a double "frill," then iron.*

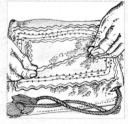

5 *Lay ric rac and ribbon onto the front of the bag alternately as shown. First pin in place, then tack carefully and finally machine stitch.*

6 *If you wish the bag to have a soft, distressed, used look, dip the whole finished bag in tea for ten minutes, wash out, hang up and dry. Put the slippers in the bag, pull the cord and pack away.*

LAVENDER POMANDERS

*T*HESE POMANDERS are simple and easy to make and are an inventive variation of the traditional clove-spiced oranges. Make them as modest presents for friends, hang them decoratively in a linen closet, pile them loosely in a dainty basket or perhaps suspend them from differing lengths of pretty ribbon at a small window.

MATERIALS

3-in. cotton (or polystyrene) balls

Pencil to hold ball

Mauve paint

Paintbrush for paint

White glue

Paintbrush for glue

Dried lavender flowers

3¼ ft. of chiffon ribbon

1 Pierce the cotton ball with a pencil to hold the ball firm. Paint the whole ball with mauve paint to match the color of lavender flowers. Allow to dry.

2 Coat the ball with glue and then roll it in a bowl of dried lavender flowers. Press into the flowers firmly until the ball is well covered. Allow to dry.

3 Tie the ribbon around the ball, dividing it into quarters, and glue it into the hole made by the pencil. Make a "busy" bow with a collection of loops, adding one longer loop for hanging. Secure all into the glued hole at the top. Allow to dry before hanging.

POTPOURRI RECIPE

INGREDIENTS

1 crushed cinnamon stick

Half a teaspoon ground cloves

Half a teaspoon ground nutmeg

1 oz. orris root powder

3 drops lavender oil

2 drops bergamot oil

1½ oz. lavender

4 cups mixed blue mallow, rosemary, thyme, meadowsweet, and lemon balm

1 In a small box mix the cinnamon, cloves, nutmeg, and orris root powder. Add the essential oils and rub between your fingers to ensure the oils are well mixed into the dry ingredients.

2 In a separate bowl place all the remaining dry ingredients. Mix together and then mix in the spices, orris powder fixative, and essential oils.

3 Store in an airtight container for about six weeks to ensure the fragrance permeates the potpourri and becomes mature. Transfer to a pretty bowl and decorate with dried flowers.

LAMPSHADES

❧━━━✦━━━❧

OIL LAMPS and dim gas light were superseded in the 1880s by the incandescent gas mantle and shortly afterward by the incandescent electric bulb. These bright lights inspired a new style for the Victorian parlor; gone were the days of soft pools of light in a richly cluttered room. A new taste for more simple design was emerging. These pretty lampshades are simple to make using ready-made shades.

SCALLOP-EDGED

MATERIALS

Lampshade 6 1/2 in. high, with
bottom diameter 11 in.

Stiff white paper, approx. 24 × 18 in.

Tracing wheel

Hole punch

White paper glue

Double-sided adhesive tape

1 Take the paper shade off the metal shade frame to use as a template. Lay the shade onto stiff white paper and extend the new shape beyond the bottom, making a scalloped edge by drawing around a cup rim.

2 With a tracing wheel, press firmly over a soft surface (e.g. an old magazine) through the paper around the scalloped edge and along the line of the old shade edge. With a hole punch, make a hole in the middle of each scallop.

3 Cut a smaller-scale scalloped edge to match at the top rim of the shade. Pierce with the hole punch and trace an embossed line to match the bottom rim.

4 Attach the top rim scallops to the shade with paper glue and when dry fasten the shade around the frame, securing it at the join with invisible double-sided tape. It may be necessary to glue the paper shade to the metal rim at the top.

LACE AND RIBBON

Lace and ribbons were two essential items in a Victorian lady's sewing box, and here they are used in a creative and really effective way. The "lacy" ribbon is, in fact, a punched paper ribbon, commonly available in the nineteenth century.

MATERIALS

Lampshade 6 1/2 in. high, with bottom
diameter 7 in.

Pale mauve (lavender) paint

Wallpaper paste

5 ft. of punched paper lacy ribbon

Craft knife

6 1/2 ft. of 1/2-in.-wide blue and
white gingham ribbon

2 With a craft knife cut 2 slits at the top and bottom of the shade all the way around between the lacy paper ribbon strips. The slits will be wider apart at the bottom than the top.

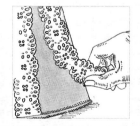

1 Paint the shade pale mauve, and allow to dry. Mix wallpaper paste and use it to paste 7 lengths of paper lacy ribbon vertically onto the shade.

3 Thread the ribbon behind the lace and through the slits between. Tie in little bows at the front of the lampshade.

PILLOWCASE AND NAPKINS

*D*OMESTIC ETIQUETTE was important in the Victorian household, so a variety of cutlery, china, and table linen was kept for different culinary occasions. When serving tea, the table was daintily set and tea-time napkins were often prettified with a lace trim.

PILLOWCASE

*T*his delightful child's pillowcase would make an ideal christening present. It is still possible to buy Victorian linen and lace in excellent condition, although modern lace is often indistinguishable from old. This pillowcase is made from a combination of new and old material.

MATERIALS

Small linen pillowcase 20 × 13 in.

Ornate lacy tray cloth 10 × 16 in.

7 ft. of crochet lace 1½ in. wide

Needle

White thread

NAPKINS

MATERIALS

Pretty, old napkins 12 in. square, with an embroidered posy in one corner if possible

5 ft. of soft lace 1 in. wide

Small needle

White thread

Sew the lace around the edge of the napkin with small neat stitches, taking care to gather the lace around the four corners so that it lies flat. To finish, the napkin may be starched and ironed.

1 Pin and tack the tray cloth onto the center front of the pillowcase. Machine stitch in place, then remove tacking.

2 With small neat stitches, hand sew the lace around the edge of the pillowcase. Make two tucks at each corner to ensure the lace lies flat. Finish off neatly to disguise the join.

3 Starch and iron and fill with a fine down pillow.

*H*OW TO LAY A TABLE

Dinner, being the most important meal, is worthy of first place. Special attention must be paid to the table-linen which must always be perfectly clean, and free of creases. Serviettes may be folded in various shapes, the mitre being one of the most popular. This shape is only suitable for plain serviettes, and the bread-roll may be placed inside. Lace-edged napkins are usually folded in a fan shape and put in the tumblers.

Mrs. Beeton's Household Management

LACE FIT FOR A QUEEN

❧⨳❧

Queen Victoria favored Devonshire lace and in 1840 she ordered her wedding dress to be decorated with handmade Honiton lace. A Mistress Jane Bidney was given the task of gathering a team of one hundred of Devon's best lacemakers to work on the dress. Typical designs on Honiton lace were floral, including roses, thistles, and shamrocks. Around 1880 rose blossoms and leaves with raised veins and edges were popular.

THE NAMING OF HONITON LACE

◌ ⋅ ◌

A Mrs. Davey, who ran the lace shop in Honiton, received an order for a dress of Devonshire lace from Queen Charlotte, the wife of King George III. She called on many of the lacemakers of Devon to make the lace, using the long-lost art of mounting fine sprigs on a handmade net. The lacemakers delivered their work to her shop in Honiton, and so the Devon style of lacemaking got its name.

◌ ⋅ ◌

LAVENDER CANDLES

✦

WAX CANDLES were expensive and used only in the grander houses or when visitors were expected, Tallow candles were chiefly for servants' use, although these too had to be used sparingly. Here is a lovely way to decorate wax candles with stems of dried lavender. Large candles have been used because they last a long time and provide a generous surface to work on.

MATERIALS

Dried stems of lavender

3 wax candles: 3 × 5 in., 2 × 6 in.
and 2¹⁄₂ × 4 in.

Wax glue

Small double saucepan

Small paintbrush

Dipping can 3 × 8 in.

2.lb. paraffin wax beads

Deep saucepan

*Never choose your
women or your linen by candlelight.*

English Proverb

*My candle burns at both
ends;
It will not last the night;
But oh my foes, and oh my friends —
It gives a lovely light.*

A Few Figs from Thistles
EDNA ST. VINCENT MILLAY

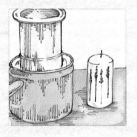

1 Sort out some good straight stems of lavender and cut them approximately ¹⁄₂ in. shorter than the candle they are to be stuck onto.

2 Melt a little wax glue over hot water in a small double saucepan. With the small paintbrush put spots of the melted glue onto the candle where the lavender will be placed. It dries quickly, so you may need to apply more glue while you work. Press the lavender onto the candle for a few seconds while it dries.

3 Continue sticking the lavender around the candle with this method, leaving between ¹⁄₂ and ³⁄₄ in. between each stem and varying the heights.

4 Put the dipping can full of paraffin wax beads into a deep pan of very hot water. The wax will reduce as it melts. Do not cook the wax. It is ready for use as soon as it is melted.

5 Holding the candle by the wick, dip quickly in and out of the hot wax. You need only dip twice; the more coats you use, the less colorful or visible the lavender becomes.

LAVENDER BUNDLES

NEWLY WASHED and ironed laundry was in the domain of the housekeeper; it was she who counted, checked and arranged it in the linen closet. Loose bundles of lavender were often placed between the layers of linen, from where they could impart their fresh clean scent. Here a generous bunch of lavender has been gathered together and tied with a rich purple wired ribbon. Such ribbons are widely available and their wire edges make it easy to tie, adjust and mold a sumptuous bow that will retain its shape.

HOW TO TIE A WIRED BOW

1 *Arrange the ribbon into two loops, and hold one in each hand.*

2 *Fold the right loop over the left.*

3 *Fold the left loop over the right, under and through the hole, pull and tie into a bow.*

And still she slept an azure lidded sleep
In blanched linen, smooth and lavendered
While he from forth the closet brought a heap
Of candied apple, quince, and plum, and gourd.

The Eve of St. Agnes
JOHN KEATS

DRIED FLOWERS

1 Fit the styrofoam into the bottom of the creamware bowl; cut to size if necessary.

URING THE long winter months, when fresh flowers were not available, garden flowers, which had been collected and dried during the summer in airy potting sheds, were arranged into beautiful floral displays. They were often protected under the characteristic glass domes so popular at the time. If you would like to dry your own flowers, collect loose bunches just before they are at their best. Bind the stems and hang up to dry in a warm airy place. The modest arrangement shown here is suitable for display on a windowsill, small shelf or mantelpiece.

2 With stems of approximately 2 in., push the heads of the African marigolds into the styrofoam around the edge of the bowl.

Roses are red, Lavender's blue, If you will have me, I will have you.

MATERIALS

Semispherical styrofoam

Creamware bowl

20 African marigold heads

Large bunch of double feverfew

Large bunch of dried lavender

3 Now make an inner circle of the double feverfew, making sure it is tightly packed against the marigolds.

4 Fill the large circular space in the middle of the display with lavender. It is easier to push in 4 or 5 stems together.

5 Pack the lavender in tightly until there is no space left. Check the arrangement carefully and make sure that all the flowers are even.

LACY-EDGED SHELVES

*T*HE VICTORIAN desire to prettify everything also extended to the humbler quarters of the house. The kitchen furniture, namely shelves and sideboards, was often lined with patterned papers and sometimes this lining was extended into a lacy edge to the shelf, which it decoratively overhung.

MATERIALS

Large sheet of recycled paper (white)
Scissors
Pencil
Small jar lid as a template
Pinking shears
Hole punch
Small sheet pink paper
Brass upholstery tacks
Pin hammer

1 Cut a number of strips of the white paper 3 in. wide. The number will depend on the length and number of shelves to be decorated.

2 Using a pencil, with the small round template touching one edge of the paper strip, draw a semicircle. Keep drawing semicircles along the strip.

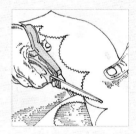

3 Cut around this line carefully with pinking shears.

4 Punch a hole in the middle of each "scallop" or semicircle.

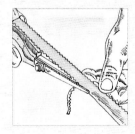

5 Cut ³⁄₄-in.-wide strips of the pink paper and "pink" both sides.

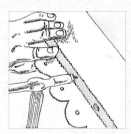

6 Lay the white paper straight side to match the top edge of the shelf, then lay the pink strip just below and fasten firmly to the shelf edge with brass upholstery tacks.

*T*he labels on the glass storage jars have been made by photocopying and enlarging old cartouche designs, which are available in source books of copyright-free designs. These are then carefully cut out and stuck onto the jars. Try writing the names of the grains, cereals, and pulses on the labels with Victorian copperplate writing.

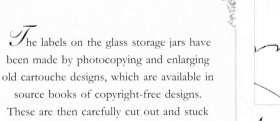

POST OFFICE NOTICE ST. VALENTINE'S DAY

It is desirable that Valentines containing, for instance, Cut Flowers, Bouquets, Confectionery, Fancy Articles &c., intended for transmission by Parcel Post, should be carefully packed by the senders so as to secure them from injury during transit.

My son is my son till he gets him a wife But my daughter's my daughter all the days of her life.

English Proverb

VICTORIAN CARDS

*T*HE VALENTINE ritual has its roots in pagan times, but the modern celebration commemorates St. Valentine, a Roman priest who was executed for his faith in A.D. 270. He became the patron saint of lovers after his last act, a letter sent to his jailer's daughter signed "from your Valentine." Victorian ladies created their own individual Valentines in which they included poems and messages, often displaying elegant penmanship.

MATERIALS

Victorian facsimile scraps
Small scissors
Cream cardboard
Paper glue
Pinking shears
Deep purple card
12 in. of glittery metallic ribbon 1 in. wide

1 Choose and cut out a pretty Victorian scrap; a young girl holding a posy of garden flowers has been used here.

2 Stick the scrap centrally onto the cream cardboard cut to 3 × 4 in. Pink the edges of the cardboard with pinking shears.

3 Stick the cream cardboard onto purple background cardboard cut to 3½ × 5 in. Cut the edges into scallops, marking the edge by using a coin as a template.

4 Make two ribbon-sized slits on the left of the card. Thread the ribbon through and tie into a pretty bow. Trim ribbon ends at an angle.

CHRISTMAS CARDS

*O*riginally a German tradition, the sending of Christmas cards was introduced to England in the nineteenth century by Prince Albert, Queen Victoria's husband, and it soon became a well-established practice. There is a wide choice of Victorian scraps available with Christmas images. These are much richer in detail and color than any contemporary designs. Here scraps have been used on a festive gold cardboard background that has been mounted on a piece of maroon cardboard. The design has been finished off with emblems from a gold doily and metallic gold braid.

Christmas is coming The goose is getting fat…

TUSSIE MUSSIE

THE TUSSIE MUSSIE, a tightly bound posy of fragrant herbs and flowers, was commonly carried in the sixteenth century to disguise unpleasant smells and protect the bearer from the risk of disease. With the development of drainage and better hygiene in Victorian times, this practical use was abandoned and tussie mussies became popular as gifts. Make your own tussie mussies according to the seasons in your garden, as presents or commemorations of special occasions, or just to symbolize the enduring intimacy of friends.

A fresh tussie mussie will last about a week in water and may be dried afterward by hanging it upside-down in a warm airy place.

MATERIALS

The herbs and flowers in this tussie mussie have been picked from a summer garden.

1 Start with a small posy for the center and encircle it with a variety of contrasting herbs and flowers.

2 Bind the flower stems tightly with florist's wire as you go, adding little bunches of lavender throughout.

3 Gradually build up the layers, keeping the posy tight by binding the florist's wire around the newly added flowers.

4 Finish by encircling the tussie mussie with an outer ring of a large-leaved herb or, as in this case, small stems of curry herb. Bind to finish.

A tussie mussie should contain several sweet-smelling herbs. The name goes back to 1440 when it occurs in the first English–Latin dictionary: "Tyte trust or tusmose of flowers or other herbs = olfactorium." Tussie mussies are obviously similar to the highly scented nosegays carried by judges. In the Colonies, ladies would carry them to church on Sundays, and in Victorian times they were sometimes used to send a message through the symbolism of flowers.

PIN CUSHION

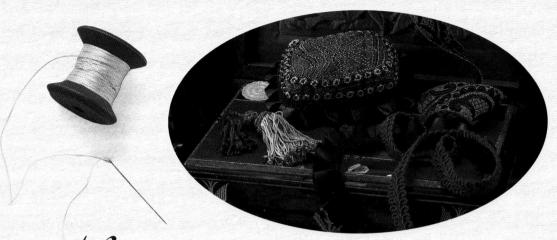

NEEDLEWORK WAS an important aspect of a Victorian lady's list of accomplishments. The sewing box was common to all homes, containing pins and needles made of steel, which were expensive and rusted easily. Airtight ivory or bone needlecases became popular, and in order to conserve their precious pins, women designed and fashioned the most exquisite pin cushions.

She will surely be undone, who wears a pin in her Bridal Gown.

English Proverb

MATERIALS

1$\frac{1}{2}$ ft. of woolen paisley

6 in. of polyester wadding

28 in. of pleated black ribbon-edged braid

3$\frac{1}{4}$ ft. of small-beaded braid

Black thread

Steel pins

1 Cut the paisley fabric into pieces: 2 pieces 5 × 4 in., 2 pieces 5 × 2$\frac{1}{2}$ in. and 2 pieces 4 × 2$\frac{1}{2}$ in.

2 Pin and tack together into a rectangular "box" shape, leaving open one side.

3 Turn the right way out and stuff with polyester wadding until the cushion is quite firm. Sew up the side.

4 Sew black braid around the sides like a "skirt."

5 Sew two rows of the beaded braid around the perimeter of the cushion.

6 Make a flower pattern and border with steel pins, by pushing them firmly into the cushion.

DÉCOUPAGE HAT BOX

HATS WERE an essential part of every woman's wardrobe, from scullery maids to ladies of the highest rank. It was important that they were stored carefully in hat boxes to protect them from dust and sunlight.

Découpage was a favorite Victorian craft. Use this technique to make an authentic-looking hat box that, in "the absence of any hats," could be a very useful storage box.

... it is not that artistic power has left the world, but that a more rapid life has developed itself in it, leaving no time for deliberate dainty decoration, or labours of love.

The Drawing Room and its Decorations
MRS. ORRIN SMITH 1877

MATERIALS

Large circular box with lid (cardboard or plywood), 14 in. in diameter, 7 in. deep

Dull blue paint

Paintbrush for paint

Small scissors

Ladies' fashion cuts for découpage

Wallpaper paste

Paper lace

Crackle glaze (water-based) stages 1 and 2

Paintbrush for crackle glaze

Rag

Burnt umber oil paint

Polyurethane satin-finish varnish

1 Paint the box blue. Use *two* coats to ensure good cover.

2 With a small pair of scissors carefully cut out a selection of black and white ladies' fashion engravings.

3 Mix the wallpaper paste, and paste the cutouts onto the sides and lid of the box. Paste strips of vertical paper lace onto the side of the box between the fashion cuts. Paste the frilly-edged lace around the top, bottom and lid rim of the box. Allow to dry.

4 Paint stage 1 of the crackle glaze onto the box (following the manufacturer's instructions). Allow to dry. Paint stage 2 of the crackle glaze. Dry it quickly with a hair dryer and the cracks will soon appear.

5 With a rag, rub in the burnt umber paint to fill in the cracks. Wipe off excess paint with a clean rag, holding it as flat as possible so as not to pull the pigment out of the cracks. Allow to dry and varnish with two or three coats of polyurethane varnish to protect.

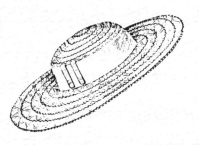

*Blond lace may be revived by
breathing upon it, and shaking and flapping it.
The use of the iron turns the lace yellow.*

Enquire Within
Upon Everything 1894

The cosy fire is bright and gay,
The merry kettle boils away
And hums a cheerful song.
I sing the saucer and the cup;
Pray, Mary, fill the tea-pot up,
And do not make it strong.

The Poets at Tea, "Cowper"
BARRY PAIN 1864–1928

TEA TIME

*I*T WAS the footman's job to serve tea upstairs. For everyday purposes a tray was brought to the drawing room and tea was laid out on a small table. This lovely découpaged tea tray will give you great pleasure to use and is simple to make. It has been effectively antiqued to give it a Victorian look; black and white flower engravings have been used along with scrolls, both photocopied from source books of nineteenth-century botanical illustrations and decorative borders.

MATERIALS

Metal tray

Oil-based metal primer (if tray is unpainted)

Water-based lilac paint

Paintbrush for paint

Small pointed scissors

Prints of botanical illustrations and scrolls or other source material

Wallpaper paste

Crackle glaze stages 1 and 2

Burnt umber oil paint for antiquing

2 rags

Polyurethane satin-finish varnish

Paintbrush for varnish

Turpentine for cleaning varnish brush

A young girl who puts sugar in her tea after pouring the milk will surely stay a spinster.

English Proverb

1 Paint the tray with the metal primer. If it is already painted, after a light sanding apply two coats of lilac-colored paint.

2 With the small scissors carefully cut out the botanical illustrations and scrolls.

3 Apply the paste to the tray and stick the prints down, easing out any trapped air bubbles. Apply the scrolls to the edges and center.

4 Apply the crackle glaze, stages 1 and 2. The second coat may be dried with a hair dryer to encourage the glaze to crackle more quickly.

5 Rub burnt umber paint into the cracks with a small rag. Wipe off the excess with a clean rag.

6 Allow to dry and finish off with at least two coats of polyurethane varnish. For a really smooth finish lightly sand the penultimate coat.

*M*UCH ATTENTION was paid to the care
of the Victorian wardrobe. Dresses for special
occasions were made of a great variety of exquisite
materials and trimmings, and needed to be carefully
stored and hung. The soft padding of this coathanger
encloses a fragrant quantity of dried lavender flowers,
the traditional fragrance for closets. The little sachets
made to match, with their fresh lavender scent, will
help to keep the moths at bay.

LAVENDER COATHANGERS

MATERIALS

2 wire coathangers

10 in. each of gray and purple shot silk

10 in. of polyester wadding

2 handfuls of dried lavender flowers

Matching thread and needle

3¼ ft. of lace for trimming the gray hanger

20 in. of lace for trimming the purple hanger

12 in. each of silk checked ribbon and mauve silk ribbon

1 Lay the coathanger onto the silk and cut a double length, half as long again as the hanger, 3½ in. wide.

2 Cut the wadding slightly longer than the hanger and wrap around. Before sewing it up loosely, fill with dried lavender.

3 With the hanger inside the silk, turn under a ½-in. hem. Slot the lace between the seam, pin, then sew with running stitch, gathering the thread every 4 in.

4 Finish off neatly at the handle, then bind the handle with similar-colored ribbon and tie with a wired bow.

LAVENDER SACHETS

MATERIALS

Off-cuts of the same silk as used for the coathangers

3¼ ft. each of fine lace and broderie anglaise for the trim

Needle and thread

Lavender flowers

Ribbons in a faded color to match the silk

1 Cut silk into shape: square 4 × 4 in. or circle 4 in. in diameter.

2 With right sides together, enclosing the gathered lace or broderie anglaise into the seam, stitch with small stitches or machine the seam, leaving a 2-in. opening.

 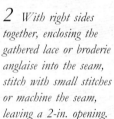

3 Turn inside out, fill with lavender flowers and finish off the opening neatly. Tie a small bow and sew in place.

BOTTLES

❦ERBS AND flowers have been used over the centuries in the making of cosmetics and to this day they remain important ingredients in health and beauty preparations. Many of these recipes have been handed down from mother to daughter through all ages and cultures. Perfumed floral waters, lavender being a particular favorite of the Victorians, have refreshing astringent qualities, and when decanted into pretty glass bottles they become delightful accessories to grace a lady's dressing table.

LAVENDER WATER

INGREDIENTS

One cup lavender flowers and leaves
Airtight container
1½ cups cider vinegar or white wine vinegar
A fine sieve
Pitcher
¾ cup rosewater

1 *Put the lavender flowers and leaves into the airtight container and pour over the vinegar. Put the lid on and allow to infuse for about three days in a cool dark place; shake twice daily.*

2 *After three days, strain the lavender through a fine sieve into a pitcher.*

3 *Add the rosewater to the lavender infusion and stir to mix thoroughly.*

4 *Decant into pretty bottles and tie with wired silk bows for a really sumptuous effect.*

ESSENTIAL OILS

Essential oils are pure, concentrated essences of plants that are prepared by distillation. This is a lengthy and laborious process that requires much knowledge and skill. Very large quantities of flowers are needed to produce very small quantities of oil. The housekeeper and still-room maid were party to this knowledge in the nineteenth century and used essential oils in the preparation of oils, tinctures and ointments. Nowadays it is more practical to buy them, since they are so readily available. A few drops in a bath creates a wonderful fragrance and is therapeutic.

❦is Aunt Jobiska made him drink,
Lavender water tinged with pink,
For she said, The World in general knows
There's nothing so good for a Pobble's toes!

The Pobble who has no Toes
EDWARD LEAR 1812–88

LAVENDER-SCENTED MASSAGE OIL

Simply add eight drops of lavender essential oil to a proprietary blend of unscented massage oil. Mix two oils together for a richer scent. Try rose and lavender, and violet and jasmine.

LACY BEAD COVERS

*I*N THE summer months, when tea was regularly taken in the garden on fine days, perhaps as a refreshing break during a game of croquet or tennis, pretty lacy beaded crochet covers were used to keep dust and insects from falling into pitchers of homemade cordial, milk or cream, or bowls of sugar. They were also used to cover bowls of food in the pantry.

*T*he pretty beaded covers shown here have been made by using a crocheted edge to attach a row of glittering colored glass beads to antique doilies. The number of beads used depends on the circumference of your doily. For the large beaded cover (diameter 9 in.) with the pink and clear glass beads, you will need 24 pink and 24 clear beads. For the smaller cover (6 in.) you will need 32 blue beads, alternately opaque and clear.

MATERIALS

Selection of colored glass beads with large central holes

White crochet thread, approximately the same gauge as the existing doily

Number 12 crochet hook

Antique crocheted doilies

Of course, your ladyship knows that such lace must never be starched or ironed. Some people wash it in sugar and water, and some in coffee, to make it the right yellow colour; but I myself have a very good receipt for washing it in milk, which stiffens it enough, and gives it a very good creamy colour.

Cranford
MRS. GASKELL
1810–65

1 *String the correct number of beads onto the crochet thread.*

2 *Crochet loops of 12 chains, slipping a bead onto the chain before joining it to the edge of the doily.*

3 *Continue with these 12 chain loops around the circumference until all the beads are threaded on. Finish off neatly.*

LACY PICTURE FRAME

THERE WERE always many images to frame in the Victorian household. And with the invention of photography and the new advances in the printing industry, all families could now afford to hang a whole range of family portraits. This simple frame has been decoratively enhanced by carefully cutting and pasting a lacy paper doily onto it.

MATERIALS

Picture frame 10 × 13 in. with
front border 3 in. wide

This frame has $\frac{1}{2}$-in. raised bands on the inside and outside
edge of the front

Brick-red paint

Paintbrush

Small sharp scissors

Assortment of square and rectangular doilies

Wallpaper paste and brush

White paper

Pinking shears

Polyurethane varnish

Brush for varnish

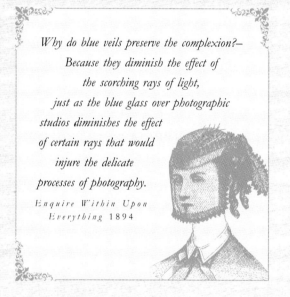

Why do blue veils preserve the complexion?—
Because they diminish the effect of
the scorching rays of light,
just as the blue glass over photographic
studios diminishes the effect
of certain rays that would
injure the delicate
processes of photography.

Enquire Within Upon
Everything 1894

1 Paint the frame with two coats of brick-red paint.

2 Cut out sections of a paper doily so that they fit around the frame neatly.

3 Arrange the pieces of doily around the frame. Paste the frame and stick the doily in place. Smooth out any air bubbles with your fingers.

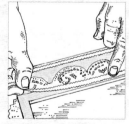

4 Cut strips of white paper on both sides with the pinking shears and paste onto the rims of the frame.

5 Finally, varnish with two or three coats of polyurethane varnish. Lightly sand the penultimate coat to achieve a smooth finish.

One picture is worth
a thousand words.

Chinese Proverb

CORNUCOPIAS

❧

$\mathcal{A}$LL MANNER of delicious and appealing desserts, sweetmeats, crystallized fruits, and bonbons were served with the coffee after an excellent meal. These little gold paper cornucopias are lined with pretty patterned paper and trimmed with paper lace and ribbons to make them into mouth-watering offerings.

MATERIALS

Template (see page 144 for an example that can be reduced or enlarged)

Sheet of gold cardboard

Sharp pencil

Scissors, large and small

Printed patterned paper (gift wrapping) for lining

Wallpaper paste

Double-sided tape

Scraps of white paper for trimming

Pinking shears

Hole punch

Pink paper lace

FRINGES AND BRAIDS

∞

$\mathcal{M}$ake a variety of cornucopias and vary the decorative edging. Try using fringes or braids. A folded length of paper that has been "pinked" vertically into a fringe is particularly effective. Make a special flourish with a glittery ribbon and bow to finish.

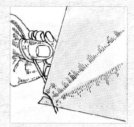

1 Draw around the template with a sharp pencil. Be careful not to scratch the gold card. Cut out with the larger scissors. Use the small scissors to cut the point as shown.

2 Lay the template onto patterned paper, draw around it and cut out. With the wallpaper paste, stick this paper inside the gold cardboard. Allow to dry thoroughly.

3 Bend the cardboard around and lay a strip of double-sided tape on one side of the cone shape. Bring the other side around and evenly over the tape. Press to stick firmly.

4 Trim back the opening on the top so that the final contents are more easily revealed.

5 Using a small round template (e.g. a film canister) draw a scalloped edge on a white paper strip. Cut out with pinking shears to create a decorative edge. Punch holes in the center of the scallops and then stick around the opening with double-sided tape, lining up the join with the seam on the back of the cone.

6 Finish off by sticking

on pink paper lace in the same way. Leave it partly protruding over the edge and fold and stick back inside the cone. This makes a neat edge and disguises the cut rim of the cone.

ROSE POTPOURRI

*U*SED THROUGHOUT history, no scent is more evocative of a summer garden than the rich, heady perfume of a rose, the most traditional ingredient of all potpourri recipes. It was in the eighteenth century that the term potpourri came to mean a fragrant mixture of herbs, flowers, and spices used to decorate and perfume houses. A well-appointed Victorian home had pretty bowls or baskets of highly scented and home-prepared potpourri displayed in all the important rooms. There is nothing to surpass the wonderful faded, papery quality of dried rose blooms; use a subtle mixture of reds, pinks, and scarlets laced with oakmoss, or combine your colors to create a more vibrant or busy mixture.

MATERIALS

1 tablespoon ground cinnamon

1¼ oz. orris root powder

7 drops of rose essential oil

3 drops of cottage garden mixture essential oil

1 vanilla pod

5 cups mixed dried rose petals, buds and blooms

1 oz. oakmoss

1 oz. lavender

1 oz. lemon verbena

Small handful of whole cloves

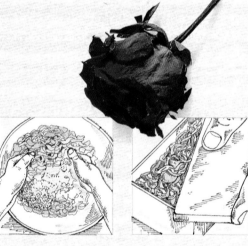

1 In a small bowl mix together the cinnamon, orris root powder, and essential oils.

2 Rub the mixture between your fingers, making sure that the oil penetrates the mixture evenly.

3 Cut and split the vanilla pod into small pieces and mix together with all the remaining ingredients in a large bowl. Remember to put aside some oakmoss, rosebuds, blooms, and petals for the surface decoration.

4 Add the mixture of fixative (orris root), spices, and oils to the bowl of dry ingredients. Stir together to produce an evenly scented mixture.

5 Put the mixture in an airtight container and place it in the dark for three weeks, occasionally shaking the container. The longer you leave the mixture, the stronger the fragrance will become. Eventually remove it from the airtight container and display in a favorite bowl.

BOOKMARK

*B*ooks in the Victorian household were treasured possessions. They usually had marbled endpapers, and it was common for the owner of the book to paste a personal decorated book plate at the beginning. Bookmarks were often of embossed leather, but a silk or satin ribbon or tasseled braid was a more appropriate marker for a book of sentimental poetry. This sumptuous gold and black braid and tasseled bookmark is simplicity itself to make.

MATERIALS

9 in. of ornate gold and black braid 1½ in. wide

Fabric glue

Gold tassel

1 Fold over the top end of the braid and secure it with fabric glue. Do not use too much glue or it may be visible from the front of the bookmark. It may be necessary to hold the braid until the glue is firmly set.

2 Turn over ¾ in. at the other end of the braid. Before gluing in place, make a small hole in the center along the fold.

3 Thread the tassel cord through this hole, spread a small amount of glue under the folded hem and press firmly until the glue has set.

4 Turn the two corners over at 45-degree angles to make a pointed edge where the braid meets the tassels. Glue and hold until set.

BOOK PLATE

*W*ith the use of photocopying it is so easy to make a collection of personalized book plates. The one shown here has been hand colored and "antiqued" by painting with a weak coat of black tea.

1 Select an appealing black and white engraving; a basket of roses has been chosen here. Cut it out and paste it onto white paper.

2 Cut out a border to frame the basket of roses. Remember to leave enough space below for the lettering and name to be inscribed. Miter the corners carefully and stick down.

3 Cut out, assemble and place Ex Libris letters in position. If you have access to a word processor it is very easy to design and print this type. Photocopy the image several times. It is at this stage that you may want to enlarge or reduce the size of your image.

4 Paint the book plate with tea, and allow to dry. If the paper crinkles slightly, iron it flat with a medium hot iron. Hand-color the basket of flowers and frame with colored pencils and paste the finished book plate into your favorite book.

MATERIALS

Selection of black and white engravings of borders, flower basket and lettering

White paper

Spray mount adhesive or paper paste

Weak tea

Colored pencils

Elphinston: *What, have you not read it through?*
Johnson: *No Sir, do you read books through?*

SAMUEL JOHNSON 1709–84

*Each book that a young girl touches should be
bound in white vellum.*

JOHN RUSKIN 1819–1900

LOVE LETTERS

> *My Darling, be a wife, be a friend, write good letters, do not mope, do not torment me.*
>
> ANTON CHEKHOV 1860–1904

HE ART OF letter writing was much practiced by the Victorians, and most people were expected to write a beautiful hand. The introduction of the penny post in the early 1840s made the sending of letters altogether much simpler, and affectionate letters were exchanged between women friends. Love letters needed to be kept secure, however, and what prettier way than by tying with a faded pink satin ribbon and sealing the contents from prying eyes with sealing wax?

MATERIALS

3¼ ft. of faded pink satin ribbon

Small piece of tinfoil

Stick of blue sealing wax

Matches

Coin or embossed head of upholstery tack

1 Tie the ribbon around the bundle of letters as shown, and knot at the top.

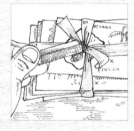

2 Put a piece of tinfoil under the knot to protect the letters from the heat of the wax. Light the wick of the sealing wax and drip the hot wax carefully onto the knot.

3 Working quickly, before the wax cools down, press the embossed surface of the coin or upholstery tack onto the warm wax to make an impression.

4 Cut the ends of the ribbon at an angle as shown.

LETTER RACK

*T*HIS DELIGHTFUL and practical découpage letter rack is just the thing to grace your writing desk. Letter racks made from wood or strong cardboard are available ready-made from most good stationery stores or are easy to assemble from craft suppliers. Wrapping paper, made from Victorian facsimile wallpaper designs, has been used along with a crackle varnish to give the letter rack an authentic feel.

It may sound like being over particular, but we recommend persons to make a practice of fully addressing notes etc., on all occasions.

Enquire Within Upon
Everything 1894

MATERIALS

Wooden or cardboard letter rack

Victorian-style wrapping paper

Scissors

Wallpaper paste

White glue

Crackle glaze stages 1 and 2

Paintbrush for glaze

Raw umber oil paint

Rag

Polyurethane matt-finish varnish

Paintbrush for varnish

Fine sandpaper

1 Cut the paper into pieces slightly larger than each side to be covered. Start with the center panel. Snip along the curved edge of the paper to be applied to the three curved panels.

2 Mix the wallpaper paste and apply to the surface of the letter rack. Carefully smooth the paper onto the central panel front, taking care to smooth out any bubbles with your fingers. Turn over the snipped edge and paste firmly to the back of the panel. Cover the back with a piece slightly shorter and cut into a curve to hide the snipped "turn over."

3 Repeat this process with the front and back panels and continue to paper all sides inside and out. Allow to dry, then cover the base in the same way and stick to the bottom of the letter rack with white glue.

4 Apply the crackle glaze in two stages, following the manufacturer's instructions. After the second coat, when the glaze has crackled, rub a small quantity of raw umber oil pigment into the cracks. Rub off the excess and allow to dry.

5 Varnish with three coats of polyurethane varnish and sand the penultimate coat lightly before applying the final finishing coat.

DÉCOUPAGE BOX

DÉCOUPAGE, a craft with a long history, became a very fashionable occupation in the nineteenth century. Technical developments in printing made it possible for everybody to collect great varieties of printed and embossed colours, images and scraps. These were avidly swapped between friends and pasted into albums and onto boxes, screens, trunks, frames, and book covers, as well as having many other applications. Victorian scraps are still available today and it is relatively easy to find a choice of shapes and sizes of blank wooden or card boxes to decorate.

MATERIALS

Hexagonal box

Green paint

Paint brush

Victorian scraps – bride, roses, and butterflies

Scissors

Wallpaper paste

Paste brush

Sheet of orange or pink recycled paper

Pinking shears

Polyurethane satin-finish varnish

Paintbrush for varnish

Fine sandpaper

He had 42 boxes, all carefully packed,
With his name painted clearly on each
But, since he omitted to mention the fact,
They were all left behind on the beach.

The Hunting of the Snark
LEWIS CARROLL 1832–98

 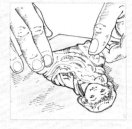   

1 Give the box and lid two coats of green paint. Allow to dry.

2 Cut out the scraps carefully and lay them onto the lid of the box to plan your design. Remove, then paste the surface of the lid and stick the first scrap in place.

3 Paste the roses to one side of the figure and the butterflies to the other.

4 Cut a strip of the orange or pink paper 2 cm (³⁄4 in.) wide. Make a zigzag edge on one side with the pinking shears and cut a scalloped edge on the other with ordinary scissors. Paste around the edge of the lid, overlapping the side.

5 Add more "pinked" paper strips to decorate around the base of the lid and the bottom of the box. When thoroughly dry, varnish with three coats of polyurethane varnish, sanding the penultimate coat to achieve a smooth finish.

PAINTED BOXES

*A*ny one of this appealing assortment of decorated boxes would make a lovely gift, perhaps containing homemade sweets or jewels, a shell collection, ribbons, or sewing equipment. Or you could fill a rose-adorned, heart-shaped, beribboned box with deliciously scented pot pourri. Here is how to make a painted box with combed paint decoration.

MATERIALS

Oval box

Cream paint

Dark blue paint

Decorator's rubber comb

Paintbrush with a pointed end to its handle

Polyurethane satin-finish varnish

Paintbrush for varnish

1 Paint the box with two coats of cream paint. Allow to dry. Paint on the blue paint and, while it is still wet, comb the pattern into the paint, revealing the cream paint underneath.

2 Scratch squiggles in between the combed sections with the sharp end of the paintbrush handle. Allow the paint to dry and varnish with three coats of polyurethane varnish.

DECORATIVE KEYS

THE HOUSEKEEPER, as head of the Victorian household, carried her symbol of office, the châtelaine, hung with the keys to the still room, linen and store cupboards, about her waist. The jangling of the keys warned any inattentive underservants of her approach. Beautiful tassels are surprisingly easy to make in many different threads, shapes, and sizes and they look very effective when attached to a special key, perhaps for a writing desk, linen closet or jewel box.

MATERIALS

1 skein each of green and orange thread twist embroidery thread

Small amount of cotton batting

Needle

16 in. of gold cord

The key of India is in London.

BENJAMIN DISRAELI
House of Lords
5 MARCH 1881

1 Wind the green and orange thread a number of times around your fingers held flat. The more times you wind, the thicker the tassel will be.

2 Slide the thread from your fingers and wind some orange thread around the tassel one-third of the way down; tuck in the end.

3 To enlarge the size of the head, push some cotton batting in with a blunt needle. Stuff the head evenly and bring the thread around the cotton batting to hide it. Insert the cord at this stage, hiding the join in the head.

4 Thread some orange thread and work blanket stitch all around the head, working each row into the previous row. Decrease the number of stitches as you reach the top. Finish and push the needle through the tassel to finish.

5 Knot the cord close to the head of the tassel and, finally, trim the loops at the base of the tassel so that the ends are even.

DÉCOUPAGE KEY FOB

FOR LESS SPECIAL, but equally important keys, a lovely découpage key fob is ideal. These are quick to make from thin plywood or are commonly available from craft shops and hardware stores. They can be decorated with a variety of pretty Victorian scraps.

MATERIALS

Wooden key fobs
Fine sandpaper
Terracotta paint
Paintbrush
Victorian scraps of flowers
Scissors
Wallpaper paste
Paste brush
Polyurethane satin-finish varnish
Paintbrush for varnish

"There's an accident" they said. "Your servant's cut in half, he's dead!" "Indeed!" said Mr. Jones, "and please Send me the half that's got my keys."

Ruthless Rhymes for Heartless Homes
HARRY GRAHAM
1874–1936

1 *Lightly sand the fob to make a smooth surface. Paint the fob with two coats of paint. Allow to dry.*

A golden key can open any door.
English Proverb

2 *Cut out your scraps carefully. Paste the surface of the fob and press each scrap firmly down in the center, smoothing with your fingers to ensure no air bubbles are trapped. Allow to dry thoroughly.*

3 *Varnish with at least three coats of polyurethane varnish to protect. If you want a more antique look, tint the varnish with a minute quantity of raw umber oil paint.*

ROSEBUD HEART

*D*URING LONG cold winters when it was nearly impossible to find fresh flowers, the Victorians arranged garden flowers that had been picked and dried in the summer months to make lovely floral displays. Dried roses and rosebuds are available from good florists or you can pick and dry them yourself. These charming little rosebud hearts can be scented with rose oil and hung in the linen closet to impart their heady fragrance, which is so evocative of an English garden.

MATERIALS

Approximately 25 tiny pink closed rosebuds

5 slightly more open deeper pink buds

Rose essential oil

20 in. of flexible wire (garden wire is ideal)

Pliers (long-nosed)

Two 20-in. lengths of light and dark pink chiffon ribbon

… be but sworn my love, and
I'll no longer be a Capulet …
What's in a name? That which we call a rose
By any other name would smell as sweet.

ROMEO AND JULIET
WILLIAM SHAKESPEARE
1564–1616

1 *Put all the rosebuds in a small bowl and sprinkle 7 drops of rose oil onto them.*

2 *Bend the wire into a heart shape, so that the ends of the wire meet at the top of the heart.*

3 *Begin to thread the rosebuds onto one half of the heart by pushing the end of the wire gently through the thicker base of each bud. After every four or five tiny buds, thread on a larger one. Complete one side of the heart.*

4 *Now thread a symmetrical number of buds onto the other side of the heart. Join the wire firmly at the top with the pliers.*

5 *Tie the double ribbon over the wire join and arrange all the buds so that their bases face into the heart and the tips of the buds are visible from the front of the heart.*

ROSETTE

*W*ith a needle and thread gather together a 6-in. length of delicate lace into a rosette. Sew into the center of the heart over the wire join. For a pretty finishing touch, attach a tiny rosebud to the middle of the rosette. Hang the heart as decoration on a bedroom or dressing-room wall or slip over the wire handle of a coathanger that holds your favorite outfit.

HAIR COMBS

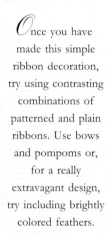

$\mathcal{F}$ASHION WAS followed with great diligence in Victorian times. Combs, ribbons, lace, and hats were carefully chosen to match and complement the day's outfit. These beautiful ribbon-adorned hair combs are directly inspired by some examples from Victorian ladies' fashion magazines.

MATERIALS

1 flat-topped button approximately 1 in. wide

12 in. of rainbow-dyed wire-edged ribbon 1½ in. wide

Needle

Thread

34 in. of dip-dyed burnt orange ribbon 1½ in. wide

16 in. of shot silk orange ribbon 2 in. wide

Hair comb with two long prongs

Florist's wire

1 Lay the button onto a 1½-in. length of rainbow ribbon. With the needle and thread, gather the ribbon edges together at the back of the button and finish off tightly.

2 Gather the remaining rainbow ribbon into a rosette by securing one end and pulling the fine wire along the edge. Sew a seam at the join. Sew the button onto the rosette.

$\mathcal{O}$nce you have made this simple ribbon decoration, try using contrasting combinations of patterned and plain ribbons. Use bows and pompoms or, for a really extravagant design, try including brightly colored feathers.

3 Fold the dip-dyed burnt orange ribbon into three loops. The middle loop, placed behind the other two loops, needs to be 1¼ in. longer. Sew in place behind the rosette.

4 Fold the shot silk ribbon in half and sew it behind the previous three loops, with the ends slightly apart. Cut V shapes to finish off the ribbon ends.

5 The ribbon decoration may now be sewn onto the comb, if the comb has conveniently placed holes to sew through. If not, it is probably easier to attach with soft fine florist's wire.

6 Take the wire between the two short folds and one long fold of burnt orange ribbon and wind three times around the top of the comb. Twist to secure and then tuck the wire ends out of sight.

*Only God,
my dear,
Could love you for
yourself alone
And not your
yellow hair.*

Oedipus at Colonus
W. B. YEATS
1865–1939

EASTER EGGS

THE EGG IS a potent symbol of creation, and the decoration of eggs at Easter has become a universal Christian tradition. In Central Europe real eggs are stunningly decorated in a number of ways; they are etched, batiked, engraved, painted or beaded, each one bearing the individuality of its maker.

MATERIALS

Papier mâché Easter egg case
Collection of glittering sweet wrappers
Scissors
White glue, very slightly diluted
Small paintbrush
3¼ ft. of gold ribbon 1 in. wide
3¼ ft. of gold ribbon ½ in. wide

The papier mâché egg cases used here are easy to obtain. Here one has been découpaged with a crazy patchwork of glittering candy wrappers and tied together with a sumptuous gold bow to enclose its enticing contents.

When love is declared on Easter Day A marriage is certain the following May.

English Proverb

1 Cut the glittery papers into even-sized strips slightly wider at one end. They do not need to be long enough to reach the center of the egg. Decide how you are going to place them around the egg, contrasting the color and pattern for maximum effect.

2 Start on one side of the egg. Paint the area to be covered with glue and press the glittery paper in place; turn the paper strip over the rim of the egg and stick down just inside. Continue around the egg, alternating the colors. Press down firmly to eliminate any folds or creases.

3 Stick some more paper in a crazy patchwork fashion into an oval shape in the center of the egg case and enclose it with a band of wide gold ribbon. Allow to dry. Decorate the other half of the egg in the same manner.

4 Stick the thinner gold ribbon in a band around the rim on each side of the egg. Pack with delicious Easter treats and tie with a beautiful shimmering gold bow.

The practice of giving chocolate eggs as presents at Easter was introduced to England from Germany, as were so many charming customs, during the nineteenth century. At this time exquisite papier mâché egg "cases" were widely sold. Most often they were découpaged with Easter subjects, the Easter rabbit being a favorite motif. The cases were filled with an assortment of chocolate eggs and given as presents to children on Easter Sunday.

VALENTINES CARDS

*I*N VICTORIAN TIMES most homes would have had a copy of *The Language of Flowers*, a much prized and useful little book. It was an index of the symbolic meaning of hundreds of flowers. This popular book was widely interpreted, and both fresh flowers and images of flowers, as used in Valentines, carried specific symbolic meanings. Of the flowers most commonly used to convey messages between lovers:

A rose meant "love"
A pansy meant "thought"
Lily of the valley meant "a return to happiness."

MATERIALS

Gold doily	Small pointed scissors
Large scissors	Paler pink stiff paper
Paper glue	12 pink sequins
Dark pink cardboard	Craft knife
Pinking shears	Approximately 3¼ ft. of gold ribbon
Victorian embossed scraps of flowers	Pink paper lace

1 Cut out a ring from the center of the gold doily. With the paper glue, stick this ring onto a slightly larger circle of the dark pink cardboard. Cut around this circle with the pinking shears to make a zigzagged edge.

2 Cut out the scrap carefully with the small pointed scissors. Stick carefully onto the center of the circle. Now stick this circle onto a 5¼-in. square of paler pink paper. Stick 12 sequins in place around the central motif.

3 Cut, with the craft knife, two ribbon-width slits between each sequin. Thread the gold ribbon behind the sequins and through the slits; tie into a bow at the top of the cardboard. Make a border by sticking lengths of paper lace around the outside of the square.

Accept these wishes which your maiden sends,
Ne'er may you feel the want of steadfast friends.
May health, and wealth and happiness be thine,
And may you welcome this, my Valentine,
Have I another yes, one wish in store,
That some day we may meet to part no more.

VALENTINE C.1840

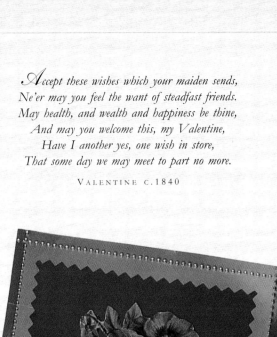

VALENTINE VERSE

Will you, won't you,
Do you, don't you
Love me, Darling Valentine?
For I love you very dearly,
And I want you to be mine.

The music of your voice
Just makes my heart rejoice,
For I know that
You are mine.
My own sweet Valentine.

A feast of flowers here behold
A thing of joy to see
But Ah! to me 'tis sweeter far
To feast mine eyes on thee.

VICTORIAN VALENTINE VERSE
ANON

ROSES AND ORANGES

*T*HIS RICHLY opulent pyramid of alternate layers of tiny kumquats and rich red dried roses will stun and delight guests. Place the pyramid in the center of the dining table for special occasions or perhaps among the delicious desserts waiting to be served from the chiffonier or sideboard.

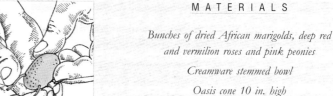

MATERIALS

Bunches of dried African marigolds, deep red
and vermilion roses and pink peonies

Creamware stemmed bowl

Oasis cone 10 in. high

Stiff florist's wire

1 lb. fresh kumquats

1 Break off the stems, leaving ¾ in. on all the dried flowers.

2 Place the oasis cone in the creamware dish. Gently, but firmly, push a row of peonies around the base of the cone.

3 Cut lengths of florist's wire approximately 4 in. long. Push the wires through the end of the kumquats, then fold the ends of the wires together and push into the oasis to fasten the kumquats in a tight row above the peonies.

*My love is like a red red rose
That's newly sprung in June
My love is like the melody
That's sweetly play'd in tune.*

A Selection of Scots Songs II 1794
ROBERT BURNS 1759–96

4 Add a layer of vermilion roses, followed by a row of marigolds and peonies, then another row of deep red roses.

5 Add a second row of kumquats and then continue building up alternate layers of the different flowers.

6 Nearer the top of the pyramid you will need to slice off the ends of the kumquats, before you thread the wire through, so that they do not stand proud of the flowers.

7 Continue with alternate layers and top with a single kumquat.

POMANDERS

*T*HESE CHARMING variations of the more well-known clove-spiced orange pomanders are quick and simple to make. They look their best piled together in a pretty china bowl. A delicious mingling of perfumed and spicy scents has been achieved by laying the pomanders on a fragrant bed of whole cloves.

MATERIALS

Oasis balls of varying sizes, the largest 4 in. in diameter

Large number of tiny pink rosebuds (usually sold by weight)

Smaller number of deep red, yellow and deep pink half-opened rosebuds

Rose essential oil

1 Push the tiny pink rosebuds one by one into the oasis ball, making sure they are tightly packed together and no oasis is visible between the buds.

2 Continue adding buds and, at regularly spaced intervals, push in a single more open, deeper-colored rosebud.

3 Continue in this manner all around the ball until it is evenly covered.

4 When the ball is completely covered, sprinkle a few drops of rose oil over the pomander.

*T*ry arranging different colored rosebuds into patterns around the oasis ball, or use in combination with other dried garden flowers.

ROSE SACHETS

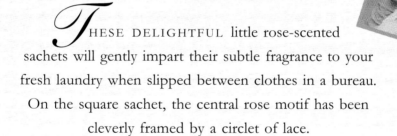

𝒯HESE DELIGHTFUL little rose-scented
sachets will gently impart their subtle fragrance to your
fresh laundry when slipped between clothes in a bureau.
On the square sachet, the central rose motif has been
cleverly framed by a circlet of lace.

MATERIALS

*3 lengths of 8 in. of fine
cotton, each printed with a
different rose design*

Needle

Thread

Rose-scented potpourri

*A variety of lace for edging,
approximately 2 ft. for
each sachet*

*Gray wire-edged, faded pink
satin and fuchsia pink silk
ribbons for bows to decorate*

*1 Cut 2 identical pieces
in each cotton of a circle,
square and diamond
shape. All should be
no more than 4 in. wide.*

*2 Turn the right sides
together and hand or
machine stitch around
the edge, leaving a 1½-in.
un-sewn gap.*

*3 Turn the sachets the
right way out and lightly
fill them with the pot-
pourri. Sew the gap in
the seam neatly.*

*4 Neatly sew the lace
around the sachets by
hand, taking care at the
corners. You will need to
gather the lace around the
round sachet. For the
finishing touch, sew on
small tightly tied bows.*

LAMPSHADE

Until the 1880s homes were lit either by dim gas lights, candles or traditional oil lamps. It was then that the wonderfully bright incandescent gas mantle was developed, followed shortly afterward by what seemed to be miraculous electric light. This exciting invention prompted the most profound change in house decoration, since furniture no longer needed to be arranged and clustered around a dim light source. A new, simple and less cluttered house style emerged that went on to become the Arts and Crafts movement. This sunny daffodil-yellow lampshade has been imaginatively adorned with lace rose motifs, used for appliqué designs in dressmaking; these are available in notions departments. Finishing with fringed braid gives the shade a very Victorian feel.

MATERIALS

Small yellow fabric lampshade, 6 in. high,
with top diameter 4 in. and
bottom diameter 10 in.
4 or more (depending on size) lace rose motifs
Fabric glue
3¹/₄ ft. of off-white fringed satin braid
20 in. of matching braid for top

Treat your friends as you do your
pictures, and place them in their best light.
JENNIE JEROME CHURCHILL
Mother of Winston Churchill

To prevent the Smoking of a lamp. Soak the wick
in strong vinegar, and dry it well before you use it;
the flame will then burn clear and bright.
ENQUIRE WITHIN UPON EVERYTHING 1894

THE LAMPLIGHTER

The installation of public street lighting was a welcome introduction to life in the nineteenth century. Gas lamps were lit at dusk by the lamplighter, a popular character whose presence was a discouragement to criminals. He would extinguish the lamps at dawn accompanied by a chorus of singing birds.

1 *Arrange the lace motifs around the center of the lampshade so that they are evenly spaced. Stick them very carefully in place onto the shade with small amounts of fabric glue (this can be easily removed if you get it in the wrong place).*

2 *Cut the fringed braid to the right length for the bottom rim, allowing a little extra to overlap in order to make a neat join. Stick along the bottom edge very evenly, making sure that the fringe hangs down beneath.*

3 *Cut the matching braid for the top edge and stick in place with the fabric glue. Pay particular attention to the join. A little extra glue here will stop the edges from fraying.*

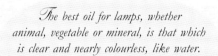

The best oil for lamps, whether animal, vegetable or mineral, is that which is clear and nearly colourless, like water.

ENQUIRE WITHIN UPON
EVERYTHING 1894

The last day in September – immensely cold, a kind of solid cold outside the windows … Don't read this. Do you hear that train whistle and now the leaves – the dry leaves – and now the fire-fluttering and creaking … Why doesn't she bring the lamps?

KATHERINE MANSFIELD
Hampstead 30 SEPTEMBER 1918

PICTURE FRAMES

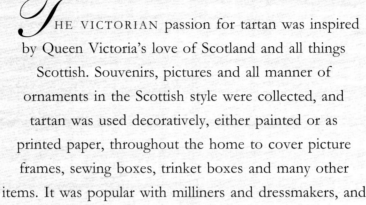

$\mathcal{T}$HE VICTORIAN passion for tartan was inspired by Queen Victoria's love of Scotland and all things Scottish. Souvenirs, pictures and all manner of ornaments in the Scottish style were collected, and tartan was used decoratively, either painted or as printed paper, throughout the home to cover picture frames, sewing boxes, trinket boxes and many other items. It was popular with milliners and dressmakers, and tartan fabric and ribbons were often woven in the finest silk. Tartan ribbons are still popular today and these picture frames have been deftly decorated with ribbons and rosettes.

MATERIALS

Picture frame 6 in. square, with a
1¾-in.-wide flat front

Dark green paint

Paintbrush

3¼ ft. of tartan ribbon 1½ in. wide

Scissors

Double-sided adhesive tape

32 in. of wire-edged purple ribbon
1 in. wide

Scraps of leather

Pinking shears

4 decorative upholstery nails

Hammer

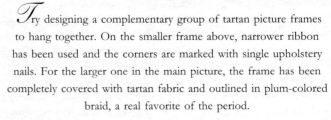

$\mathcal{T}$ry designing a complementary group of tartan picture frames to hang together. On the smaller frame above, narrower ribbon has been used and the corners are marked with single upholstery nails. For the larger one in the main picture, the frame has been completely covered with tartan fabric and outlined in plum-colored braid, a real favorite of the period.

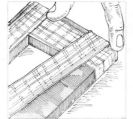

1 Paint the frame with 2 coats of dark green paint. Allow to dry between each coat.

2 Cut the tartan ribbon into four strips; it should be long enough to stretch around to the back of the frame and overlap by ³⁄₄ in. Place double-sided tape where the ribbon is to be stuck. Pull the ribbon taut and press down onto the tape, over the sides and secure it on the back of the frame. Complete all four sides in this way.

3 Cut the purple ribbon in 8-in. lengths. Secure one end of the wire that runs through the edge and pull the other to gather the rosette. Secure the wire to hold the gathers, fold back both ends and disguise the join in the folds of the rosette.

4 Cut 4 small circles of leather 1¼ in. in diameter with the pinking shears.

5 Place the rosettes on each corner of the frame and nail through the center of the leather and rosette with the decorative upholstery nail.

Guard against unnecessary over-embellishment in the decoration of small frames, so as not to detract from the image therein.

SUMMER BONNET

*L*ADIES' FASHION was of the utmost importance in Victorian times, and middle-class women possessed a hat for every season and for all manner of occasions. These were often decorated with a stunning variety of trimmings, ribbon bows, rosettes, feathers, braids, and even fresh flowers. This beautiful antique straw bonnet has been elegantly trimmed with a circlet of wide taffeta ribbon and an abundance of pretty wired ribbon roses. To achieve the faded cabbage-rose effect, shaded taffeta ribbon has been used, with a darker shade along one side of the ribbon.

BLEACHING STRAW BONNETS

Wash them in pure water, scrubbing them with a brush. Then put them in a box in which has been set a saucer of burning sulphur. Cover them up, so that the fumes may bleach them.

Enquire Within Upon Everything 1894

American ladies who wish for a kiss,
Will remove their own hat
and put on his.

MATERIALS

Straw hat with wide rim

4¾ ft. of wire-edged orange taffeta ribbon
1½ in. wide

Needle

Matching thread

Scissors

3¼ ft. of wire-edged orange taffeta ribbon
3 in. wide

A selection of wire-edged shaded taffeta ribbons in
7 colors – pinks, purples, reds and orange. Each ribbon
should be 20 in. long and 1½ in. wide

3¼ ft. of bronze wire-edged taffeta ribbon
2 in. wide

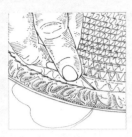

1 Bind the edge of the rim of the hat with the 1½-in.-wide orange taffeta ribbon. Very slightly gather the ribbon along the wire edges. This helps you to stitch it neatly around the curve.

2 Sew the wider orange taffeta ribbon loosely around the center of the hat. Ruckle it slightly and hold in place with tiny, widely spaced stitches.

3 To make a ribbon rose, take a 20-in. length of ribbon. Fasten one end of the wire that runs through the edge. Pull the ribbon along this wire and gather tightly.

4 Fold the end of the ribbon over and turn the gathered ribbon around on itself to form a flower shape. Use the drawn-up wire to bind the base of the "rose."

5 Make a number of rose leaves by taking a 6-in. length of bronze ribbon. Find the middle point of one side and fold the top edge either side of this middle point down over the ribbon. Turn over and fold the edges to the middle. Stitch to close and attach to the side of the rose. Sew a group of seven leaves and roses onto the back of the hat where the ruckled ribbon splits into a tail.

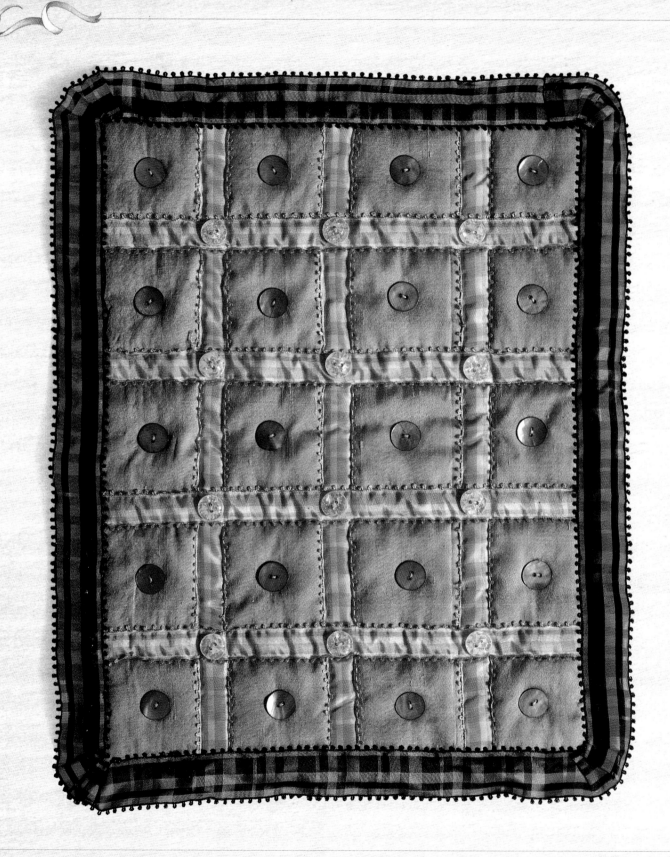

BUTTON QUILT

The NEWLY rich middle-class women in the nineteenth century who could afford to employ servants found themselves with an increasing amount of leisure time. They practiced all manner of needlework and sewing activities and generally achieved high levels of skill in a variety of techniques, including needlepoint, intricate cross-stitch, and colorful and elaborate patchwork and quilting. The abundance of ladies' periodicals published at that time provided inspiration and patterns for fashionable fancy work such as needlecases, pin cushions, and sewing caskets. Ladies' workboxes, much collected to this day, were packed with all the essential tools of an accomplished needlewoman. This quilt, criss-crossed with checkered ribbons and studded with pretty pearly buttons, makes a stylish cover for a sewing basket.

1 *Place the polyester wadding between the silk top and satin brocade back of the quilt. Lightly tack the pieces together.*

2 *Cut the pink ribbon into lengths and lay them across the quilt in an even lattice pattern. Pin and then tack them in place. Hand or machine stitch along each side of the ribbon.*

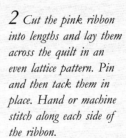

3 *Sew the iridescent plastic buttons to mark each crossing of the ribbons and sew a larger pearl button in the center of each square.*

In Germany, to protect a girl from evil spirits she should tie a red ribbon around her head, whereas in England, a silk ribbon tied around the throat will help fight disease.

CECILIA
CAVENDISH

MATERIALS

Lightweight polyester wadding 18 × 14 in.
Gray silk 18 × 14 in.
Gray satin brocade 18 × 14 in.
Needle
Thread to match ribbons and background
11 ft. of bobble-edged pink checkered ribbon 1 in. wide
12 iridescent flecked plastic buttons, ½ in. in diameter
20 mother-of-pearl buttons, ¾ in. in diameter
6½ ft. of dark pink and black bobble-edged checkered ribbon 1½ in. wide

4 *Tuck the top and back of the quilt in on itself around the edge. Hand stitch all around, making a neat seam.*

5 *Pin the darker ribbon around the outside edge of the quilt, gathering three tucks at each corner to ensure the ribbon border lies flat. Sew on neatly with black thread, turning the ends over to make a hidden join.*

GLASS PLATE

*D*ÉCOUPAGE practitioners were eager to try all sorts of inventive techniques. You can still find occasional examples of Victorian glass plates that have been découpaged from behind the glass. In fact, the whole technique is back to front: the glue is applied to the front of the paper motif, paint is applied behind the paper and all this shows through on a brilliant smooth glass surface.

'Tis the last rose of summer
Left blooming alone;
All her lovely companions
Are faded and gone;
No flower of her kindred,
No rose-bud is nigh,
To reflect back her blushes,
Or give sigh for sigh …

Irish Melodies 1821
THOMAS MOORE 1779–1852

MATERIALS

Shaped glass plate

Victorian Valentine scraps

Small scissors

White glue, diluted with water

Brush for glue

Pink paint

Paintbrush

Polyurethane varnish

Brush for varnish

SONG

Her cheeks are like roses
Her eyes they are blue
And her beauty is mine
If her heart it is true

Her cheeks are like roses
And though she's away
I shall see her sweet beauty
On some other day

JOHN CLARE 1793–1864

1 Carefully cut out 7 Victorian Valentine scraps. Make sure they are the appropriate shape and size to fit your plate.

2 Apply the diluted glue to the front of your scrap, then press it firmly into place on the back of the plate, taking care to smooth out any trapped air bubbles with your fingers. Allow the glue to dry.

3 Paint the back of the plate, covering the paper scraps with the pink paint. You will need to apply at least 2 coats. Allow to dry thorough

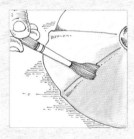

4 Apply 3 coats of varnish over the paint to protect the surface from scuffing and scratches.

*O*nly bring this plate to the table on special occasions. It is not possible to immerse the plate in water, just sponge it clean and dry with a cloth. You may prefer not to use it at all but rather to hang it decoratively from the wall with plate hangers.

INDEX

ACKNOWLEDGEMENTS

The author would like to give very special thanks to Heini Schneebeli for his care and attention to detail in taking the really lovely photographs in this book. And to all my good friends who have happily lent me beautiful objects from their own homes: Raynes Mills, Dufy Ayers, Anthea Sieveking, Marion Manheimer, Mary Port, Alan Stewart, Sophie Hedworth, Pat Schleger, Naomi Gornick, Sarah Fitzgerald, John and Sarah Carrier, Brian Pound, and my mother, Dulcie Beilin Morel; to Gloria Nichol for her constant encouragement and to Graham Day for his creative help; to Catherine Buckley for the loan of the blue satin slippers on page 77; and to Roger Vlitos for his advice on the fern-stencilled notebook on pages 38-9. Thanks are also due to Lakeland Plastics Limited, Alexandra Buildings, Windermere, Cumbria, LA23 1BQ for supplying paper doilies; to V.V. Rouleaux, Ribbon Supplies, 10 Symons Street, London, SW3 2TJ (0171 730 3125); to Chattels, 53 Chalk Farm Road, London, NW1 8AN (mail order 0171 267 0877), for supplying dried flowers; and to Mamelok Press Limited, Bury St Edmunds, IP32 6NJ, for supplying the Victorian scraps used throughout the book.

The Victorian limerick on page 31 comes from the author's own collection; *Life Below Stairs* by Frank E. Huggett, quoted on page 41, is published by John Murray Limited (1977); the cartouche designs on pages 88 and 89, and the engravings on pages 96-97 and 110-11, were photocopied from copyright-free source books published by Dover Publications.

Special thanks to Anna Bentinck for her invaluable help in finding the original Victorian material.

Very special thanks to my children, Hannah and Raphael, and to Teo Spurring, who have been so patient, understanding and supportive during the production of this book.

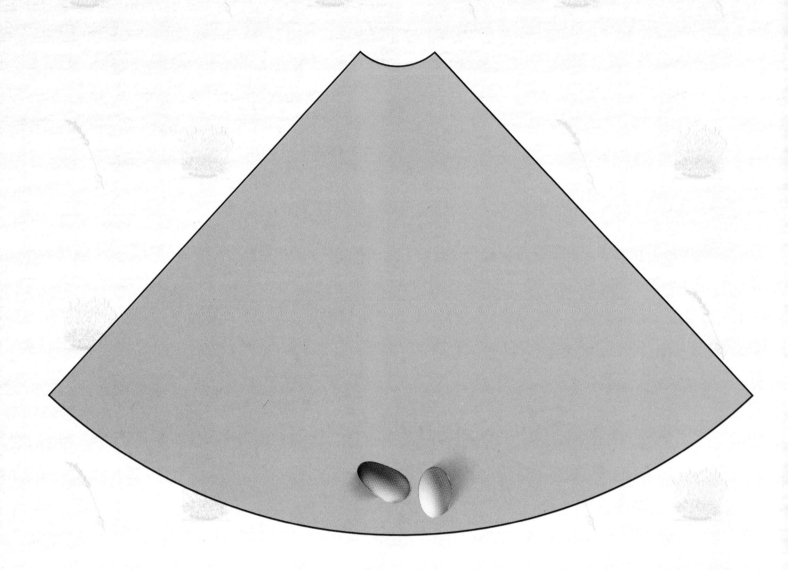

Cornucopia template (see page 106) – this can be enlarged or reduced as desired